Sarah Kay

Twelve states and a kingdom

Sarah Kay

Twelve states and a kingdom

ISBN/EAN: 9783337175078

Printed in Europe, USA, Canada, Australia, Japan

Cover: Foto ©Suzi / pixelio.de

More available books at **www.hansebooks.com**

AND A

KINGDOM.

By S. R. K.

Watseka, Illinois.
Iroquois County Times Print,
1878.

To my mother, the one true sympathizer in
every sorrow from youth to age,
I dedicate this work.

S. R. K.

PREFACE.

THERE are certain mornings dawning so bright and glorious and so filled with inspiration that my feeble pen would fain grasp the hidden revelations in the air, to insure their portrayal to the few friends most appreciative. Of the many assayed but ineffectual attempts to reduce the chaos of my thoughts to a state of form and completeness, I will not speak. But this February morning of 1877, bejeweled with frost and encircled with sunshine, when apparently Spring is negotiating with Winter for balmy air and budding foliage, comes an assurance from the land of my birth that my literary efforts have been appreciated by loving friends whose constancy has remained unshaken during the buffetings of twenty years and I am induced to commence a recital of my wanderings through "Twelve States and a Kingdom." The various guide-books compiled for the use of travelers by sea and land, have been the faithful pilots to point out to me the historical events herein mentioned and have stood as a lighthouse between me and error. Go little book! Under the flag of truth, I launch thee, trembling, upon the waves of criticism. Ere thou art entirely stranded amid the breakers of public opinion, may some few voyagers on the Sea of Literature, have derived a day's recreation as they bask in the sunshine of the most pleasant details, or sail under the clouds of which their experience is perhaps a counterpart.

CHAPTER I.

THE centennial year is a thing of the past and the anniversary of the next century will unfold its beauties to us only through our spiritual vision.

Thus ere the chirography of that happy event enacted at Philadelphia, becomes obliterated by that most prodigious of effacers, time, I hasten to chronicle my experience during my journey to, and sojourn amidst, the wonders of all climes, cast together under the broad canopy of heaven and sheltered under the municipal wing of the Quaker City. A year's wrinkles have gathered upon many a face since the final stitch was set in the garments prepared especially for this tour of the world. Those very garments that rustled and shone with all the splendor of newness, alas! have yielded up their brightness and lustre and become old. But, save the victims of war, tempest, fire, riot and confusion, were this the centennial year, America's children and her foreign brothers and sisters would set forth with the same streaming banners of their nationality, independent and free, fortified with gold, silver and greenbacks to master the infinite sight of a century's growth. Among the many trials of life, ranks foremost the making up of one's mind. If a person have decisiveness of character he is deemed fit to care for himself without adventitious aid. For a timid woman, an undertaking like the overlooking of two continents, was no small affair to decide. Being fortunately circumstanced there was no crusty husband in the case to agonizingly grasp the pocket-book and groan "economy or starvation;" but my indulgent partner lovingly lifted his eyes over the rim of his daily paper and met my suggestions for a summer's trip with a hearty approval. The fiat went forth. A *woman* had made up her mind. When a female heart is set upon a journey, woe be not him that seeks to thwart her calculations. My chaperon was "chosen, selected and sworn" not to disappoint me. Being a prosperous member of the bar of our county he would not see my legal rights infringed upon and possessing extreme sociability and sufficient knowledge of the important histronic events of the past, whose shadows we were soon to be cast under, and, understanding the transactions of the present he would be one in whose presence ennui would be unknown. With his amiable spouse tucked under one arm, the other reserved for my use in emergencies, I fancied perfect security awaited me throughout my proposed journey. Monday morning, September eighteenth, 1876, wa ' e day fixed upon for our departure. While the sultry days of August did not deter our preparations, . the cooler weather of September was hailed with satisfaction. At last everything had been reduced to a state of completeness. The gown for stated occasions had been perfected and its owner initiated into the mystery of its secret folds. Of the comforts stowed in satchel and trunk no traveling public could complain.

Every possible want had been anticipated. The last few days of our home stay began to pass heavily for our work was finished. The feminine portion of the cargo was ready to be shipped. Can I ever forget my feelings of almost childish delight when my ticket was given me, that elongated talisman that was to be my guide from "W—— to New York City and return " which were the magical words engraved thereon. The various important places we were to touch were arranged like so many coupons measuring a half yard in length, and our imagination clothed them with an interest rightfully their due. I entrusted this treasure (the loss of which would render me undone) to the most secret corner of my purse and breathed a prayer that some innate necromancy might surround it and avert my sudden ejection from the cars at some lone spot for which my inclinations were not bound. The appointed time drew near. Was there ever such happiness that the shadow of a doubt did not cloud? There was yet the parting from one I held most dear ere I could launch myself on this sea of prospective happiness. One sigh from the bosom I loved best to rest upon, effectually vanquished my carefully constructed air-castles and I realized truly that home was the dearest spot on earth to me. I gazed upon my ticket as a fatality, and danger

and endless separation seemed to be written upon each of its tags.
During the decade of our married years no such distance as this that
threatened to loom between us had ever been dreamed of, and now
I was the first to put hundreds of miles betwixt my idol and myself. The dread encompassed in those last moments at home, will
remain with me always and I can safely say, now, after a twelve
months intervention between that sad period and the present, that
I shall not voluntarily purchase another ticket which I am compelled to follow for a distance of a thousand miles without the
presence of my husband. The morning of the eighteenth of September dawned at last. There was an early meal without an
appetite; a solemn walk to the depot, a few more wretched moments of waiting and the five o'clock train hurried into our quiet
city. The steaming engine snorted and puffed as if to give vent
to its overcharged feeling, but such safety valves were denied me
and I could only breathe and act with the calmness of despair.
While husband and wife bade a hasty adieu, Mr. and Mrs. B——,
my traveling companions, cast furtive glances at our baggage lest
the sleepy agent had neglected his duty and left what should have
been aboard, behind. Of course some necessary article must be forgotten and Mrs. B—— missed her parasol as the iron horse gave a
sudden pull and moved out of the station leaving his track and
one sorrowful watcher far in the distance. During the eight miles
ride to S—— where we were to leave the Toledo, Peoria & War-
saw Railway for the Cincinnati, Lafayette and Chicago Railroad,
the long suppressed tears flowed freely and I was glad my companions were busy with each other, that, unnoticed I might indulge
my emotions and perhaps feel better for the outburst. I dried my
eyes as the cars came to a halt and said to myself, "Seraphenia it
is your duty now to compose yourself." In less than an hour we
were again on our way. Meeting a young acquaintance who
seated himself opposite us, we were agreeably entertained on our
way to LaFayette, Indiana, where he resided. His youth, combined with manliness, excited our admiration and his easy description of persons and things in general, were significant of rapid
improvement and that his time had not been thus far wasted to
have acquired so much useful knowledge ere the Rubicon of casting his first vote is safely passed; I say safely passed because
voting the triumphant Republican ticket as I am sure he will,
indicates that the political principles of this youthful editor, rest

upon a sure foundation whose corner stone is, *freedom*. We laid
hold upon his suggestion that we make the Park View hotel our
stopping place while in Philadelphia and regretfully parted his company. Our trainmen dined at Indianapolis, but some of the passengers like our trio, skirmished in the mysterious corners of their
lunch baskets for a repast of home preparing excelling all the sale
edibles exposed to view. As we neared Cincinnati I was reminded
by cornfields upon the hillsides, of dear, old New York, my own
native state with its multitudinous hills and dales so pleasing to
look upon. The western farmer, the owner of miles and miles of
prairie so monotonous to the sight, might inwardly groan at the
idea of constructing lines of stone fences across the hillside to keep
the golden pumpkins from rolling away from their mother stalk,
but how cheering to the tired traveler is the sight of the growing
grain on the hilltops upon the one side while the clay colored
water of the Ohio upon the other, discharges its vapor and becomes
dew to moisten the ripening kernel. At this stage of our progress
I bethought me of the tunnels we must pass through and I
remarked that we ought to have been provided with lanterns to
light us through the dark places and no sooner had the words
escaped me till, plunged in a deep cavern, the faces of my friends
were no longer visible and we had need of the clairvoyant's vision
to trace the character of the rocky wall that environed us. We
emerged from the darkness with smiling countenances. Is there
not an innate joyousness implanted within the heart of man when
smiles, laughter and hilariousness are indulged in even amid the
rushing of the car over rock, precipice and cataract that frown and
appal as we journey hither and thither as our restless inclinations
bid. We reach Cincinnati at five P. M. The omnibus takes us
up a small rise of ground and lands us at a pleasant dwelling
occupied by a lady friend of Mr. and Mrs. B——'s. We find our
hostess so charming in manner, with a face and form to be loved
and admired, and a disposition and management of home and
children to be envied, that we have but one regret: that is that
our stay cannot be protracted to days instead of a few hours. After
a refreshing supper we are introduced to a kind, elderly gentleman
who evidently is not averse to the attractions of our widowed hostess, and who offers to show us as many famous sights in the City
as can be seen in the short space of three hours. The statistics
that I shall herein give are just as I was informed and if there are

errors in this narrative ascribe them to hearsay as I cannot vouch for the truthfulness of all contained in these notes any farther than I can truly say I have perfect confidence in my informants and believe they gave me the the best information they were possessed of. Already my artistic "jottings on the spot" have become so blurred that they are but imperfect helps in the formation of this record, and I must rely upon memory and her twin sister, imagination, for an intelligible recital.

CHAPTER II.

CINCINNATI is situated on the north bank of the Ohio. It has a frontage of ten miles on the river and extends back three miles. The hills that surround it are about 450 feet in height. Its scenery is variegated and not equalled by any other city in the United States, so I am told. It is built upon two terraces, the first sixty feet and the second 112 feet above the river. More than one-third of its population are German, who reside principally in that portion of the city north of the Miami canal, which they have named "the Rhine." It is an entirely different country "over the Rhine," the German language alone being spoken and the signs are in German. First we are taken to the bridge across the Ohio, said to be the longest span in the world, being eleven hundred feet. The entire length is two thousand two hundred and fifty-two feet. It might properly be called "the bridge of sighs," both on account of its great proportions, and in commemoration of the twelve suicides committed from its height. Leaning over its railing we peer into the waters made dark with the shades of eventide, and watch the frail boats move in subserviance to the strokes of the oar. Head-lights like stars glimmer here and there, and I muse on all the treachery that silent sheet of water contains and wonder if the souls of those departed ones are hovering near this dreadful

2

place from which they took their voluntary flight. Have they found a better clime or are they wishing themselves back again on this very bridge from which they precipitated themselves? Death is solemn when it is inevitable but self-destruction is terrible in the extreme. It is too true that there is an almost irresistible impulse to cast one's self into the water or from any great height, and from this mammoth structure, the tendency to destroy life may be aggravated considering that the misery of the three states, Indiana, Ohio and Kentucky, and the three cities, Cincinnati, Covington and Newport which this point overlooks, may here be concentrated, and perhaps it is meet that some of the anguish may here find oblivion in the watery grave. We next visited the Probosco-Davidson fountain, also called the Tyler-Davidson fountain, one of the finest in the world, being all bronze and costing near $300,000. The work was cast in Munich. I held a little messenger in my pocket that I wished to speed on its homeward way, and finding a proper place I deposited it safely with a silent wish that it might find the loved at home, distant two hundred and fifty miles, not too weary already with waiting. But the hour of nine drew near and we must retrace our steps and seek a comfortable place in the cars that must be our lodging place for the night. No sleeping coach could be obtained and so it seemed that there were plenty of other people traveling over the Baltimore and Ohio railroad, tired and sleepy and seeking rest but finding none. The first part of the night I had a seat to myself, but about three o'clock I was obliged to resume an upright position and make room for another unhappy female. I may as well say once for all that if one derived his happiness from a crowd, the railcar at this period was the place for a full realization. Crossing the southern part of the State of Ohio in the night, Tuesday morning breakfast found us at Parkersburg, 195 miles from Cincinnati. It is the extreme south-eastern part of the State of Ohio and is a city of ten thousand inhabitants. We have passed through five tunnels since leaving Cincinnati. At Parkersburgh we cross the Ohio river on a bridge one and one-third miles long, with six spans over the river and forty-three approaching spans, completed in 1871 at a cost of over one million dollars. We again draw upon the lunch box for supplies with the exceptions of coffee which was obtained from a can in possession of a small boy who stood on a bank near the car window. At Grafton the mountain division of the road commences. This day is an

epoch in our journey and enstamped on my memory with life-long
vividness. With mountain scenery for the eye and agreeable
conversation for the ear we were doubly entertained. The magical
words rang in my ears, "we are crossing the Alleghanies." I was
seated on the left side of the car, the one most favorable for an
inspection of the grandeur before us, and my seat-mate was a
social, candid gentleman who had familiarized himself with this
mountain wildness and directed my attention to the various
wonders, grand and sublime, as we flew along on the brink of
destruction as it seemed. This day bears another noted event of
my life, the missing of my noon-day meal. Whether the loss of
appetite was caused by the curvatures in the road which rocked the
cars like a boat tossed on the waves (the effect of which we were
told to counteract by the free use of lemons with which we were
well provided) or whether the sublimity of my surroundings would
not admit of the gross masticatory proceeding, I leave my readers
to imagine for themselves, but true it is sandwich, chicken, pastry,
frosted cakes, fruit and confectionery were alike devoid of their
usual flavor, and I was filled with contemplations of the infinite
grandeur around me and might well exclaim "I have meat that ye
know not of."

Eighteen miles from Grafton we strike Cheat mountains. We
pass through the longest tunnel on our way, Kingwood tunnel,
4,100 feet long and costing one million dollars; also Murray's
tunnel 250 feet long. There is a distance of two miles between the
two. Between Parkersburgh and Deer Park, in Maryland, with
its one hundred inhabitants, there are twenty-four tunnels. The
nineteenth and twenty-fourth are the longest. Deer Park has an
altitude of 2,700 feet. Here Gen. Grant was wont to pass his vaca-
tions. During each succeeding summer's heat will my mind revert
to that lovely spot, Deer Park, on the top of the Alleghanies, with
its grottoes, springs and green lawns and above all its fine air of
which the denizens of the marshy prairies are denied. Two large
engines drew us to the top of the mountains and when the descent
began the forward one ran ahead of the train at a frightful rate and
as I gazed from the window and saw places where the road surely
must meet a rocky termination I fancied the flying monster leaping
from the track to find a lodging place only in the dim depths below.
A feeling of fear came over me such as I had never felt before. I
often ask myself the question, would I dare take the risk again?

We were entertained with such tales as that once upon a time a
certain engineer and brakesman exchanged quids of tobacco while
rounding one of the numerous curves in the road. I have heard of
the meeting of two extremes. I never saw a nearer verification
than when our engine saluted the final car of our train, (if inanimate objects can enact a salutation) and at the speed we were
going one might well fancy our iron horse endowed with nerve and
sinew and muscle to thus obey the will of man who hath said as
God spake to the sea "Thus far shalt thou go and no farther." In
many places stray drops from miniature cataracts dashed upon us as
we passed. Imagine a storm in that wild region when each tiny
rivulet becomes a mighty torrent. Laughing cascades leap from
dizzy heights and gushing springs form innocent little brooks, that,
as they murmur along their rocky bed, gather force and strength
and develop into navigable rivers. Here is the fountain head of
the Potomac that miles distant bears upon its broad bosom the
vessel of war or the boat of the pleasure seekers. The dangers we
feared were not far away and about two P. M. we were informed
that farther progress was barred by a fearful chasm made by the
washing out of a large culvert, and that in the abyss below were
heaped cars of coal and that our transit must be made on foot over
stones and planks laid on the now empty bed of the stream that
must contain a rushing tide when the rains descend, and augment
the waters to a destructive flood. The picture needs no fancy color-
ing. Our surroundings were weird enough for a fairy tale. It was
estimated that two thousand persons were congregated in that
mountain gorge. There were passengers from three trains of from
seven to nine cars each, besides the workmen employed in repairing
the break in the road. Our baggage was transferred by the hands
of the trainmen. A defile of a thousand persons through those
lonely mountains, methinks is not a scene of frequent occurrence,
but such a romantic experience was well worth the delay. On
reaching the eastern side, some seated themselves on the railroad
ties, some on logs and stones; some climbed the mountain side by
the aid of trees so thickly set they seemed to conceal every imagin-
able danger. The sound of a pistol cut the air and cries of
"Modocs" were raised to make the scene more terrifying and add
to our entertainment during the embargo. Many of the southern
and western States were represented. A bride and groom from
Oregon lent a charm to our novel position. Politics were not for-

gotten in that isolated glen and a vote being taken a delegation of
Democrats from St. Louis swelled a majority of two for Tilden. Old
Sol was fast on the decline when relief came in the form of a passenger train from the east, and then ensued a display of selfishness,
a conscientious historian may well hesitate to narrate—with the
eastern passengers hurrying off to possess the cars we had vacated
some three hours before, and the western watchers crowding on to
secure seats, for we well knew there were not coaches sufficient to
accommodate the waiting multitude. After every available space
had been seized, even to the wood-box, the remainder seated themselves in the aisle on their satchels, if they possessed them, if not
they remained standing. It was a season of equal rights—the right
to care for number one, and the heart of a president of a Woman's
Rights Association would have bounded in her bosom to have seen
strong men clinging to their seats with the tenaciousness of despair
while the fragile sex enjoyed (?) the right of perpendicularity in the
aisle with over-crowded bandboxes under their arms and convulsive
looking satchels in their hands, while the order for even *standing*
room going on below would have necessitated the services of a
chiropodist had not the conductor opportunely appeared demanding
a sight of madam's ticket thereby opening a new channel of annoy-
ance, and the corns were forgotten long ere the eagerly sought for
ticket came to the surface of one of those unfathomable hand-bags,
when, as fast as one article is removed another flies in to take its
place rendering a downward view impossible, and the contents
must be removed piece by piece as the desired article is sure to be
at the bottom. But conductors survive and grow corpulent amidst
such every day occurrences, and our sympathies need not be extended in their behalf. What bundles of magic conductors are! Un-
daunted by crowds they seem to peer into space to common mortals
invisible, for imaginary seats, so intense is their desire to cater to
the wants of the passenger. This model conductor was master of
the situation. What he did with the uncomfortable crowd I know
not, but soon there was no one left standing in the aisle and I was
even allowed a seat by myself where half reclining, with my head
to the open window, I was enabled to catch not only a cold but a
moonlight view of Harper's Ferry. The mountain that towered
above us was all the more solemn in its midnight grandeur. The
heavens were thickly set with stars which flashed out in all brilliancy and were reflected in the placid waters of the Potomac and

Shenandoah rivers. One star falling from its dazzling height, was
received on the bosom of the Potomac and forever lost. I longed
for the day light that I might the better overlook a place so full of
interest. "Point of Rocks" takes its name from a bold promontory
which is formed by the profile of the Catoctin mountains (a contin-
uation of the Blue Ridge) against the base of which the Potomac
runs on the Maryland side, the mountain towering up on the opposite (Virginia) shore, forming the other barrier to the pass." So
we read. There seemed no limit to its height as I gazed out from
the car window as far as my eye could extend. I imagined rebels
lying in ambush for our swift flying train and half expected a band
of greybacks to momentarily pounce upon us. I thought of the
war that is ended, let us hope, forever, and prayed that o'er this
region already twice battle scarred, the Angel of Peace would
henceforth hover as she reigned this night in the mountain shadows
or in the soft, stellar light from above.

CHAPTER III.

WE reached Washington our Nation's Capital, Wednesday
morning, September twentieth, at about three o'clock, tired
and weary. We followed a sable guide to the Hillman House, the
original portion of which was built by George Washington in 1776.
But at that hour in the morning and not having seen a bed since
we left home, our concern was not so much when and by whom the
hotel was built, but whether it contained comfortable lodgings.
We were placed as near the sky as the roof of the building would
admit, but as this was the centennial year I was prepared to under-
go any amount of inconvenience, and to be astonished at nothing
that might happen. My bed was clean and tolerably soft and I
slept the sleep of the just, after Mrs. B—— had settled the question
that her bed was not clean and that she had not left her downy
couch at home to be entertained (?) in Washington in such a

shabby style. The breakfast hour found me a willing complier to
its demands. The inner-woman satisfied I was ready to look about
me. It did not take a close inspection of my room to discover that
it was carpetless, and as my soles are extremely sensitive to any
contact with bare floors I decided with Mrs. B—— in favor of a
removal if no better quarters could be furnished us. The landlord
seeing that we were practical people and not to be trifled with,
accordingly placed at our disposal, large, handsomely carpeted
apartments and we settled our baggage with quite a homelike
feeling and proceeded to take ourselves out for a day's reconnoiter-
ing of the quiet city that sleeps so peacefully among its numerous
parks. It seemed to me to be filled with echoes of the past which
the rumble of the street cars but h lf awakened. I fancied the
inhabitants living upon a perpetual inheritance that necessitated no
care for future wants and left them at liberty to dream on uncon-
cerned, save as to the passage of some bill that threatened to disturb the continuance of their rest, but which eventually was "laid
on the table"—that convenient way of disposing of all unpleasant
matters a decision upon which might influence a voter in the wrong
direction when the re-election period arrived. Their lethargy may
be somewhat disturbed when the White House changes occupants
or when the too vehement tones of some orator of the Senate
Chamber, resounds through the silent halls of their dwellings. We
visited the Treasury Department, just east of the White House. It
is 582 feet long by 300 feet wide and cost six millions of dollars. It
contains two hundred rooms of whi h the finest is the cash room.
In the gold room there is usually about ten millions of dollars in
gold coin, and may be seen by a permit from the Treasurer. By
the way we had a permit from Senator Logan of Illinois to visit
this building, and I will say that on our way to Washington we fell
in company with a Mr. Davis an l son, from Cincinnati, whom we
found very pleasant c mpanion , and th y accompanied us during
this day's pilgrimage around the city. The Executive mansion or
the White House, is on Pennsylvania Avenue, one and a half miles
west of the Capitol. It is of freestone, painted white, 170 feet long,
86 feet deep, two stories high. The east room is the grand parlor
of the president, and to my eyes unused to such splendor, was fairly
dazzling in its richne s. It is 80 feet long 40 feet wide and 20 feet
high. The blue, red and green rooms are on the same floor.
Owing to some repairs being made preparatory to the reception of

Gen. Grant and family, then at Philadelphia, we only saw the blue room. I felt disappointed at not seeing a real, live president, but while we were inspecting Gen. Grant's domestic appointments, he was holding a reception at the Illinois State building at Philadelphia, it being New York's day at the centennial. I had made up my mind to shake hands and be friendly and neighborly with Ulysses and Julia as their former home, Galena, is only about one hundred and fifty miles from old Iroquois, where a portion of my bringing up was undertaken. I shall have to be content with a view of Vice President Colfax, and an opportunity to take him by the hand (which I neglected however). I shall probably see a great many men that like him want to be president but it is not possible that any republic will stand long enough to gratify every man's ambition in that direction.

The park south of the White House is lovely. In the center of the lawn is a bronze statue of Jefferson. The conservatories are on the west of the mansion. Somewhere during the day's journey we visited a statue of Lincoln, erected by the colored people. The first contribution was five dollars given by Charlotte Scott, it being the first money she earned in freedom. This statue is at the end of a street car line, and while we sat on the curb stone waiting to be conveyed thither, we fell in with a lady and gentleman on their return from the centennial. They said there were many places of interest they had neglected to visit but their stay could no longer be protracted with pleasure, and while the tears ran down the brown cheeks of that young father he said, there was one sight yet in waiting for them, far surpassing all they had seen, and that was the darling faces of their little ones awaiting their arrival home. How true ! What are worth all the results of man's inventive genius compared to the priceless jewels God sets in our homes, alas many of them only for a season, till they are recalled to form a diadem of angelic beings, fit emblems of the glory of the eternal.

CHAPTER IV.

THE chief attraction at Washington is the Capitol. I am indebted to "Appleton's Hand-book of American Cities," for the following description of the building. "The Capitol is one of the largest and probably the most magnificent public building in the world. It crowns the summit of Capitol Hill, (90 feet high) and consists of a main building 352 feet long, 121 feet deep and two wings each 238 by 140 feet. Its whole length is 751 feet four inches and covers rather more than three and a half acres. The material of the central building is a light yellow freestone (painted white) but the extensions are pure white marble. The surrounding grounds embrace thirty acres embellished with fountains and statuary, and are known as east and west grounds. The main front is towards the east and is adorned with three grand porticoes of Corinthian columns. On the steps of the central portico are groups of statuary, and in front on the grounds is Greenough's colossal statue of Washington. The bronze door which forms the entrance to the Rotunda from the east portico, was designed by Randolph Rogers, cast by Von Muller, at Munich, is seventeen feet high and nine feet wide, weighs 20,000 pounds and cost thirty thousand dollars. The work is in alto-relievo and commemorates the history of Columbus and the discovery of America. Each of the eight panels contains a scene in the life of the discoverer, and the statuettes, sixteen in number, between the panels and on the sides of the door represent the eminent contemporaries of Columbus. The Rotunda is 96 feet in diameter and 180 feet high. It contains eight large pictures illustrating American history, painted for the Government by native artists. The Dome rises over the Rotunda in the center of the Capitol. The interior measures 96 feet in diameter and 220 feet from the floor to the ceiling. A spiral stairway between the outer and inner shells afford easy access, and an opportunity of inspecting the fresco painting on the canopy over-

3

head. This is the work of Brumidi, and covers six thousand feet of space, and cost $40,000. It consists of a portrait of Washington in a sitting posture. To his right is seated the Goddess of Liberty, and on the left a female figure representing Victory and Fame proclaiming Freedom. In a semi-circle is a groupe of females representing the original sister colonies, bearing aloft a banner on which is inscribed the national motto (E. Pluribus Unum.) Surrounding this undercircle are six groups representing War, Agriculture, Mechanics, Commerce, the Navy and Science. All the figures, sixty-three in number, are of colossal proportions, so as to appear life size when seen from the floor beneath. From the balustrade at the base of the canopy is obtained a view of the city and surrounding country." You may well suppose us weary in body and limb when this height was reached. But what a grand spectacle met our view. The Potomac dotted with white sails that were mere specks in the distance beneath. Fairfax Court House was pointed out to us as being the nearest the rebels got to Washington, and the Metropolitan Methodist Church as being the house in which Grant worshiped regularly each Sabbath day; also Howard University, which was founded in 1867, for the education of youth "without regard to sex or color" but its students seven hundred in number, are nearly all negroes. The Dome is three hundred feet high, and the streets of the city center from it. "The old Hall of Representatives (now used as a National Statuary Hall) is the noblest in the Capitol. Light is admitted through a cupola in the center of the ceiling. Over the south door is a statue of Liberty, and an eagle, over the north door a statue representing History standing in a winged car, the wheel of which, by an ingenious device, forms the dial of a clock. In 1864 the Hall was set apart to receive statues of eminent Americans; each State being requested to send statues of two of its most eminent men. Moran's painting of the "Grand Canon on the Yellowstone," further adorns the Hall. We visited the present Hall of Representatives, the finest legislative chamber in the world. The Senate chamber is smaller than the Hall of Representatives, and is reached by the corridor leading north from the Rotunda, while the Hall of Representatives is south. "The Supreme Court room, (formerly the Senate chamber) is reached by the corridor leading north from the Rotunda. It is decorated with busts of the former Chief Justices. The Library of Congress was founded in 1800, was burned by the British in 1814;

was again partially burned in 1851, and went into its present room in 1853. The collection, the largest in the United States, numbers nearly 300,000 volumes, and increases at the rate of ten or fifteen thousand volumes yearly. All copyright books are by law required to be deposited in this library." We had a distant view of the Soldiers Home, (for disabled soldiers of the regular army). We read that a park of 500 acres surrounds the buildings, and that it has been the custom of the Presidents, since Pierce's administration, to occupy one of the smaller buildings of the Home as a summer resort, and here President Lincoln passed some of the last hours of his eventful term. From the Dome we had a view of the Arlington House, once the residence of George Washington Parke Custis, the last but one of the Washington family. It was later occupied by Gen. Robert E. Lee. Near the place two thousand one hundred and eleven unknown soldiers are buried. The bodies were gathered after the war from the battle fields between Bull Run and the Rappahannock. Near this is an amphitheatre with accommodations for seating five thousand persons, where are held the annual services of Decoration day. The graves of the white soldiers are separated from the colored troops and refugees, by a distance of over a half mile. Washington is situated on the north bank of the Potomac, and covers an area four and one half miles long by two and one half broad. Gen. Washington, if not the actual chooser of the site, had it selected through his agency, and it was he who laid the corner stone of the Capitol, September 18th, 1793, seven years before the seat of Government was removed from Philadelphia, and eighty-three years before our journey to the Centennial commenced. The city was laid out under Washington's directions, by Andrew Ellicott. Washington desired it christened the "Federal City," but its present name was conferred on it September 9th, 1791. "The sessions of both Houses begin at noon and usually close before sunset, but sometimes they are prolonged far into the night. A flag displayed over the north wing of the Capitol indicates that the Senate is in session; over the south wing, that the House is in session. If sittings are held in the night the great lantern over the Dome is illuminated affording a light visible for many miles." No inferior buildings, like weeds, crowd out the great flower of the Capitol. It blooms on dispensing a fragrance which the whole nation may inhale. As I sat upon its broad steps I realized that I was sheltered by a home of our forefathers building; under a roof

whose capacious width and breadth would admit and welcome the
coming of each child of our beloved republic. The lovely day drew
to a close, and we were glad to seek our commodious quarters at the
Hillman House. We were prepared to do ample justice to the
excellent supper awaiting us. The brisk waiters, whose dusky
powder was warranted "to wash," met our demands for fresh
supplies of steak and potatoes, with grins of delight, but I should
not be surprised to hear of their groaning in anguish ere the season
was over, if the on-coming tourist took up our march where we left
off with a like voracious appetite. One old darkey smiled out loud
when I told him hot water was my chief beverage. On our way
from the dining hall to our rooms, we stepped into the cheerful
parlor to see what attractions it might possess, and to inquire
whether all the sight seers were as tired as we were. We were a
jolly set of tramps, and recounted our encounters to each other with
the familiarity of acquaintances of long standing. We entirely
forgot our weariness when Mrs. P—— gave us a lively instrumen-
tal piece on the piano, and sang in her sprightly pleasing manner
"Is this croquet?" I contributed my feeble mite in the shape of
an old song, to the musicale, but on being requested to render
Moody and Sankeyism I resigned my place to an elderly lady, fat,
and fifty, I should judge, with more religion in her soul than music
in her voice. A tall, lean woman supported the right wing, and a
long, grey-whiskered, colporteur looking man in spectacles, drew
up at the left, while their miscellaneous friends brought up the
rear, and there they howled, their cracked, squeaky voices seeming
to penetrate the very walls, which was enough to disturb the spirit
of George Washington, had it been hovering near his former abiding place. The pious looking man, gazed in vain over and under
his spectacles at the notes, that, judging from the quavering
manner in which he rendered them, must have danced around right
lively before his faltering vision. We left the room but the din
followed us. We sought our couches only to dream that we were
being serenaded by a band of Choctaws, with Moody and Sankey
at their head as chief scalpers. Just what hour they laid down
their note books, and returned to camp, I can not designate, but
out of a heavy sleep I awoke to the consciousness that another
beautiful day had dawned and the mysteries of Mt. Vernon awaited
us.

CHAPTER V.

THURSDAY morning, September twenty-first, I set my foot on board a steamer for the first time. I had oftentimes meditated what my conduct would be on taking such a step, but when the decisive moment arrived I walked courageously aboard, and took my seat with all the steadiness of an old tar, and with as much unconcern as if I had been a sailor's wife for years, instead of never having been out of sight of land in all my life, and never venturing in a row boat but once, where I became so frightened with the water at a depth of two feet that I threatened to throw myself overboard if I was not taken ashore instanter. But this Mt. Vernon boat seemed so safe, and the people looked so happy, that surely danger must be confined to the depths of old ocean. As the band of harp and violins struck up, combined with the easy graceful swing of the boat, my soul awoke to joyousness, arousing my musical faculties and I was almost tempted to vie with the angel Gabriel in song, or keep step in a dance with the fairies that lightly sport on the waves. Alas! for the awakening. I am still but clumsy humanity with voice weak and feet sore. While the strains of the sweet music are echoing o'er the the waters and I am indulging in visionary speculations as to the height of the blue heavens above or the depth of the blue waters beneath, more practical Mrs. B——, intercepts the further progress of a rent in her glove by a "stitch in time" and is not troubled with the thought that while railway accidents may perhaps but set death's door ajar, the fatality of a steamboat explosion opens the hidden portals wide to the beauties of the immortal. The sun's glance, nor the wind's breath deter me from the enjoyment this trip affords. Among our passengers is a poor

man with but one eye. How is he to take in the manifold beauties
that everywhere present themselves. I have need of an extension
of visual orb, and could not bear the curtailing of a single ray of
light the windows of my soul are wont to refresh me with. The
banks of the Potomac are low and its waters much discolored with
recent rains. Alexandria meets our view and the hotel where
Col. Ellsworth met his death is pointed out to us. We pass Jones'
Point while the band insists that " We shall meet on that beautiful shore." This delightful song is followed by " Dixie," and I
feel all the old war spirit upon me. " The flag with one star " is
counter-balanced by " The star spangled banner," and North and
South had no reason to complain of the diversity of music—its
inspiring sentiments being adapted to both sections. Fort Washington is passed and we reach Mt. Vernon fifteen miles below
Washington on the Virginia side of the Potomac. Shall I ever
forget the sight of that long, solemn looking procession, as it
wended its way up the gravelly hill—while the guide at its head
repeated words that revealed to us the silent mysteries of this
sacred ground. It was a time fit for the chanting of holy
anthems o'er the graves of past events. Though their heroes
slept, their deeds yet spake and the air seemed filled with the
"spirits of just men made perfect," saintly companions of the
revered Washington. We pause before the entrance to the tomb.
Men lift their hats, women bow their heads to pay homage before
this plain, solid brick structure with gate of iron, through which
we gaze at the marble sarcophagi containing the remains of
George and Martha Washington. Some cast flowers inside the
gate and all march away saddened but purified by this short communion with the departed. The Mt. Vernon domain includes the
mansion and six acres. George Washington inherited it in 1752.
The central part of the mansion, which is of wood, was built by
Lawrence Washington; the wings by George Washington. From
his death up to 1856 it remained in possession of his descendants.
At that period it was purchased for the sum of $200,000 raised by
subscription, under the auspices of the " Ladies Mount Vernon
Association," aided by the efforts of Edward Everett. It is there-
fore the property of the nation. It is impossible for me to describe
all the ancient memoirs there collected. There is the key of the
Bastile, presented by Lafayette; military and personal furniture of
Washington, centenary chairs, and on the second floor, small, cosy

looking bedrooms containing little else than the inviting bed, and on the doors were names of different states. My curiosity was much excited as to the meaning of this and all my investigations concerning it have proven fruitless. We entered the room where Washington breathed his last breath. A fac simile of the bedstead and drapery are there, the original having been removed from necessity as a too curious public were carrying them away by pieces as souvenirs. I sat at Washington's favorite window and looked out upon the landscape that years ago refreshed his weary eyes after hours of mental labor, planning for the safety and prosperity of our government. Our boat load so filled the house that the small rooms were almost suffocating. It was a relief to breathe the fresh air on the lawn in front of the mansion overlooking the Potomac. What perfect rest there was under those grand old trees and what fragrance was diffused from the well-kept greenhouse. We paused under a magnolia tree planted by Washington's own hand. We were forbidden to pluck the leaves from the branches, but might gather the fallen ones, and how eagerly we sought among the green grass for the beautiful foliage of this wondrous tree. Not finding a leaf myself, a fellow traveler presented me with one which I treasure as a precious momento of the Father of our Country. We drank the clear, cold water from the deep old well whose curb was sheltered under a porch and guarded by an old colored man, who drew up the crystal beverage for every one that thirsted. He showed us a row of low, one-story buildings which in the days of our republic's infancy were the quarters of the negro servants belonging to the Washington estate. The lunch prepared in our western home not yet being exhausted, Mr. and Mrs. B—— and myself chose a cool spot under Washington's favorite oak, from which to take our mid-day meal. I gathered pebbles from a miniature gulch worn near the roots of the historic oak, and have since placed them among my few treasures at home. The magnolia leaf adorns the portrait of Lincoln, and when my thoughts would grasp the glory of two such benefactors of our country, I glance at the picture and its faded green leaf upon the wall of my dwelling. As we were masticating our food and ruminating upon the past and present, we caught sight of an advancing host that had but just landed, and soon were greeting the welcome faces of our western friends, faces now so begrimed with the smut of travel that they were scarcely recognizable, save by their smiles accom-

panied by hearty hand-shakings. But the hour for the departure
of the first boat drew near and each passenger straggled down to the
boat-landing as best suited his inclinations, and when the signal
was given we were all on board ready to depart. Shades of Mount
Vernon! I have sometimes heard the expression used in jest. To
me the words will ever suggest a day replete with a subdued, holy
happiness, a day that was as an oasis in the desert of life—such a
day as comes only to those who by work and toil know how to
appreciate calm and quietude.

CHAPTER VI.

WE left Washington Friday morning, September 22d, for
Philadelphia. Our last night's stay saw the Hillman
House filled to overflowing, and even the parlor floor was covered
with sleepers. The rail cars are no better, and we jam into our
seats. The coaches are very handsome on this line, the arms of the
seats shining like silver. I begin to doubt the propriety of buying
a return ticket, considering the manner in which I am jostled from
side to side, sometimes nearly submerged by the crowd, there will
be nothing left of me to get home with the last tag of my ticket.
My seat mate between Washington and Baltimore was chief repre-
sentative of a race of taciturn people, (which race it is to be hoped
will become extinct before the next centennial arrives). We
dashed by so many beautiful things that I longed to know just
where we were, but if I ventured a query his moroseness chilled my
inquisitiveness, and I left him to his morning paper, but oh how I
wanted to speak my mind. He wore good clothes and feigned city
airs. He no doubt thought I was from the country, in my sober,
sensible linen suit. Well, I was from a region where people are
taught courtesy and affability. Lacking these qualities no person
need simulate the true gentleman. We saw tracks of the late army

through Maryland. After a two hours ride we reached Baltimore, distant from Washington thirty-eight miles. It is situated on the north branch of the Patapsco river, fourteen miles from its entrance into Chesapeake Bay. The Baltimore and Ohio Road possesses the interest of having been the theatre of some exciting scenes during the late civil war, it having suffered severely by the destruction of its rolling stock, track and bridges. As we passed through Baltimore I thought of a certain father residing within its precincts, who sent out his two sons to battle with life, well fortified with this worlds goods; the one met with an early death—the other with moral destruction—the latter fate to be the most lamented. Our train was rolled through this city by attaching horses to the cars. Seven horses drew two cars while the lash was not spared. The streets are narrow, the houses dirty and dingy. In front of a clothing store I saw a live individual standing beside a dummy that was arrayed in fine raiment and I thought the knobby countenance of the headless man quite as expressive as the other. Chesapeake harbor was full of boats. It finally took seven large, eastern horses that would flounce down in our western sloughs, to draw one car up the grade. It is not often one has a buggy ride on the cars. I think I have the countenance of the average southerner very well impressed on my memory. Suffice it to say it is black as the blackest in the emancipated race, specimens of which thronged the streets of Baltimore, and in the white race among the lower classes, red predominates and blank ignorance stares you in the face. Perhaps we are too much governed by our prejudices in comparing different localities. I have no doubt but what this city that evidently puts its worst side out to the railway traveler, has many cultivated citizens dwelling in grandeur and who utilize this colored element in their offices and households, but I should want the waters of the Chesapeake to overflow them even forty days and forty nights before I made a valet or chief cook of any of the specimens I saw.

Humanity is well balanced. Selfishness, egotism and pomposity on the one side and affability and kindness on the other. I will sell out cheap whatever interest I may have in "My Maryland." Some parts of the state reminded me of the sloughy, shrubby land of my own county. A vote is taken on the cars at this point, and the name of Hayes is heard on every hand. The result is fifty-three for Tilden and one hundred and thirty for

4

Hayes, and this in a southern country filled with Democrats. How
my cheek burned with shame to be passed indifferently by without
being asked for an expression of opinion as to who should be ruler
over a nation women help to uphold. The Susquehannah river
empties into the beautiful Chesapeake Bay at Havre De Grace.
We cross the river on a bridge nearly a mile in length. After so
much rain all the waters are of a clayey color. Delaware is a
lovely little State with many fine sites for building. Deleware Bay
is an enchanting sheet of water. Four miles from Newark the
train crosses the famous Mason and Dixon's line, long the boundary between the Northern and Southern States. Wilmington is
the chief city of Deleware. Chester, fourteen miles from Philadelphia, is the oldest town in Pennsylvania, having been settled by
Swedes in 1643, and four miles from it, is the Brandywine, famous
for the battle fought on its banks in September, 1777. When we
are within thirty-five miles from Philadelphia, a train of palace
cars pass us, having left Washington an hour after we did. Its
splendor flashed upon us as for a second and was gone. At two
and a half o'clock, P. M., we reached Philadelphia, distant from
Baltimore ninety-seven miles, and from Washington one hundred
and thirty-five miles. We have now traveled nine hundred and
sixty miles since we left home. We take a carriage and ride a
distance of three miles to the Park View Hotel, situated on the
corner of 29th and Poplar streets, opposite Fairmount Park with
its lovely three thousand acres. We enter the hotel parlor and
negotiate with the proprietor of the establishment for a week's
board and lodging. Owing to the foolish desire of humanity to all
visit the centennial show at the same time we did (and it was
estimated that there were then one hundred thousand visitors in
the city) we were glad to be shown a small room, the floor of which
was covered with matting and the furniture of pine, painted a
light color, and consisting of two bedsteads, one wash-stand, a
table and two chairs, all new, however. A dividing line between
the two beds was formed by a white screen that, had it been
painted green might have been an indication that inside was kept
a "sample room," or what means the same thing—a place where
beer and high-wines are dealt out. I chose the birth behind the
screen in case of an invasion by burglars I might readily find
shelter in the closet opening at my right hand. For the use of
this coop we were each to pay one dollar per day, our meals to be

served on the European plan. Our trunks were brought up and it was the first sight we had had of them since leaving home. They answered well the purpose of seats though they filled up the space to such an extent that there was not sufficient room left in which to oscillate a feline; that difficulty was overcome however, as like one of Dickens' characters we had no occasion to swing a cat. We were now in a land where musquito nets were unused and it was the evening duty of Mr. and Mrs. B——, the one armed with a slipper while the other held a lamp, to lay siege to the few buzzing insects that sat upon the walls of our fortress. Entrenched behind my screen I could overlook the works with all the security of a quarter-master, who has naught to guard but clothing and rations. On our way to the hotel the carriage was crowded and our ears were regaled with the varied experiences of the company. Some had sat in a depot all night being unable to find rooms. One train, coming in from North Carolina, had tipped over and three cripples from the wreck helped to fill the conveyance. I felt as if life hung by a thread as I gazed at their bruised heads and the crutches by which they must be supported while "doing the centennial."

CHAPTER VII.

SATURDAY morning, September 23d, I arose before six o'clock but owing to a want of appetite, caused by excitement, ate but sparingly of breakfast in the large dining hall of the Park View House. We thought we were the early birds to catch the first omnibus out to the Exhibition grounds, one mile distant, but we found several heavily laden hacks and numerous burdened street cars had already proceeded us. "The Exhibition buildings are located in Fairmount Park at the head of Girard Avenue, which leads directly from the heart of the city to the main entrance. The grounds embrace 236 acres with an average elevation of over one

hundred feet above the adjacent Schuylkill. The Pennsylvania and
Reading Railroad each have an immense depot adjoining the
grounds, and as the tracks of these roads connect with every other
line entering Philadelphia, visitors arriving by rail are landed at
the gates without change of cars. There are seventeen entrances
to the exhibition grounds. The first of the buildings reached coming from the city is the main building, costing one million six hundred thousand dollars, and is one thousand eight hundred and
seventy-six feet long, and four hundred and sixty-four feet wide,
covering an area of nearly twenty-one and one-half acres. Towers
seventy-five feet high rise at each corner of the building." In constructing the building there were used eight million pounds of
iron, besides glass and wood. In order to see the sights in this
wonderful structure eleven and one-third miles must be traversed.
The total cost of the Centennial Exhibition is estimated at eight
million five hundred thousand dollars. There are seventy-five
acres of ground under cover within the main inclosure, being an
excess of twenty-five acres over the Vienna Exposition grounds.
The last named Exposition exceeded this in cost by one million
three hundred and fifty thousand dollars. Ten millions of visitors
were estimated as attending the Philadelphia Exposition, while the
attendance at Vienna was seven million two hundred and fifty-
four thousand eight hundred and sixty-seven. There were seventy
thousand exhibitors at Vienna and sixty thousand at Philadelphia.
My personal experience at this grand show that can come but once
in a life time, is as follows: On reaching the inclosing fence which
is three miles in extent, we entered at one of the seventeen entrance
gates. Additional entrance gates are provided for the exclusive
use of employees and those entitled to free admission. It being
Saturday the admission fee was but twenty-five cents. On entering the main building I could not repress a sigh born of the
thought—is one life of sufficient duration to master so prodigious
a sight? but, my dear readers do not be alarmed for I am not
going to recount a millionth part of what I saw. No tongue has
the loquacity to utter praises, no pen the mightiness of portrayal,
no one mind the comprehensiveness to grasp the intricacies of this
wonderful combination of beauty, utility, gorgeousness and grandeur. The Japanese contributors to the panorama seemed to have
anticipated the hot season by sending fans of all shapes and designs,
which first attracted my attention. I find the first memorandum

on my note-book was made while I was sojourning in Norway, and is in commemoration of the marriage of a Norwegian couple. The figures were so true to life that I supposed myself standing beside breathing creatures, till I became aware that they were the center of attraction in that vicinity, and a closer scrutiny revealed their inanimateness. Then there were Swedish groupes, one representing a mother pleading with the father for their daughter's lover, who stood bashfully in the corner awaiting the result of the intercession. In Australia was a gold monument representing thirty-five million dollars. I noted a wingless bird from New Zealand, that existed before the island was inhabited by man. Then there was the Moa bird now extinct—a coin twenty-six hundred years old—stones from Solomon's palace—crocodiles and stuffed animals of all descriptions. I saw a diamond necklace worth thirty-five thousand dollars—an adjustable sleeping apartment resembling a trunk, shutting up in a very small compass, and costing two hundred dollars; a bed-stead seemingly wrought of fine gold, worth twelve thousand dollars; a small Malachite table, price two thousand four hundred dollars. I take the following description of this one from a little tract that was given me while I was admiring the beauty of the tables of green and blue. "Malachite, Green Carbonate of Copper, emerald-green, light and dark green. Found only in the Ural mountains, in the mines to a depth of six hundred feet. These mines being under water, have not been worked since the last twenty years. Lapis Lazuli, Azurestone, Ultramarine, Lazure blue in all degrees of the height, found in granite and granular lime stone in Siberia, at the Baikal lake, and in Bucharie. The price thereof has enormously risen in the last years up to one hundred rubles per pound. Ultramarine, the most precious color is made thereof. It is used for inlaid work and jewelry. Porphyry is found at Tazilek, in the Ural mountains, and at Olonetzk in Northern Russia. The above are specifically Russian stones, which at public request, have been described. There are still the Siberian Amethyst and smoky topaz, which are the most precious and beautiful. These stones can be ground and cut only with emery and diamond dust, and it requires an amount of patience, only to be found in a Russian workman, and the manufacture thereof may well be termed one of the most ungrateful occupations. This is perhaps, why there is no competition. Among others we have exhibited a pair of small Nephrite vases, the grinding of which

alone required five months time." I scarcely knew which to
admire most, the tables of blue or green, but their prices put them
all beyond my reach. There was a mantle-piece of Malachite
inlaid with Jasper and other precious stones, valued at six thousand five hundred dollars. Large Malachite vases in Etruscan and
Roman styles, worth four thousand five hundred dollars; a piece of
Malachite weighing one thousand and eighty pounds, whose value
was four thousand eight hundred and sixty dollars. There were a
pair of vases of Lapis Lazuli at two thousand dollars. It would
require a palatial residence of much spaciousness to be adorned
with these mammoth vases without the ornaments appearing bur-
densome. There were various tables with solid gilded bronze legs,
valued from one hundred and twenty to two thousand four hundred
dollars; also a variety of clocks, albums, jewelry &c., all from
Hoessrick & Woerffel of St. Petersburg, Russia. There was a
Spanish building so real, one might fancy himself in the streets of
Spain. "Egypt, the oldest nation in the world, sends Soudan its
morning greeting to the youngest nation," were the words engra-
ven over the entrance to that ancient looking structure which be-
spake the Bible and the days of the Israelites. What shall I say
of the display of porcelain, glassware, a suite of rooms elegantly
furnished, laces, silks, velvets and furs, (Russia excelling in the
three articles last named)—historical representations from the
Scriptures both in sculpture and painting. A groupe consisting of
a Laplander, wife and baby, arrayed in robes of thick fur and just
ensconcing themselves in the farther corner of their sledge, to which
was attached a fine reindeer; also another scene, "the death of the
reindeer," were very impressive. There was a painting of Christ
fresh from the manger, with the attendants gazing in wonder, it
appeared to me, at his astounding size and agility. I should have
judged it to be a picture of a child two years of age, squirming
from the bath, but there was really beautiful statuary portraying
Our Master from his infancy to his crucifixion. There were large
pictures deft fingers had formed of highly colored worsteds, that
rivaled oil paintings in their beauty and completeness. There
were quilts whose silk foundations were one solid mass of rich embroidery of garlands of flowers in manifold designs. This, our first
day was spent in carefully and attentively canvassing a great portion of the main building. Though the pouring rain threatened a
damper on our amusements and spoiled our good clothes at the

outset, we were cheerful amid the difficulties, and at noontime
sought the "Dairy" where we were refreshed with a warm substantial dinner. When we were under shelter of the main building,
the rain fell with no unmusical sound. We ventured out long
enough to take a three miles ride around the grounds on the
narrow guage, double track steam railway. The car seats were
dripping with water that had beaten in from the open sides of the
coaches, and many of the passengers sat on the back of long seats
that ran across the width of the car. In fact the cars were very
much like the open street cars in Chicago. We registered at the
Illinois State building, which was a commodious cottage, comfort-
ably furnished for the accommodation of the citizens of that State.
It was the only place where I enjoyed the warmth of a fire while I
was in Philadelphia. Our postmaster, whose office was in that
building, was one of the most gentlemanly officials I ever met with.
The people generally volunteered information to each other, and
the policemen were extremely courteous, fulfilling the scriptural
adjuration to "be patient and long suffering." They answered all
questions with dignity and politeness, humored the querulous,
guided the lost to places of safety and guarded well the rich treasures entrusted to their care, rigidly insisting that the motly crowd
refrain from any manipulations of the dazzling stores so temptingly
arrayed, as to invite touch as well as sight. Being neither a man
nor a minor I was not attracted by the mineral ore only in the extent of display which was vast. It was a splendid sight after as-
cending the spiral stairway, to look down upon the objects animate
and inanimate; the former moving with slow tread that the eye
might be enabled to encompass all the loveliness; the latter pre-
senting a combination of bright and sombre hues enchanting to the
beholder. When weary we ensconced ourselves in the easy chairs
and divans placed there for our use, and watched these children of
curiosity gratify their love for the beautiful as they marched along,
pausing here and there for a closer examination of some one article
more remarkable than another. When thirsty, our parched
throats gratefully received the cooling draught from a magnificent
soda fountain. Our first day at the Exposition is ended and too
tired for expression we "hang on by the eyebrows," as some one
expressed it, to a crowded street-car while the rain deluges the
occupants of the platform. Fastidiousness may as well be laid
aside in such a place. No exceptions are made in favor of race.

color or previous condition, in a street-car where humanity is so
compact that none but a conductor capable of materializing and
de-materializing ad libitum, dare effect an entrance.

CHAPTER VIII.

SUNDAY morning, September twenty-fourth, I awoke and
found the rain still pouring which bespoke for tourists a
dismal day. We were told it had rained for two weeks. If you
have ever been far from home in a strange city, waiting for the
sun to shine and waiting in vain, you will give me your sympathy
during the trials of that Sabbath, in Philadelphia. I fear I must
acknowledge home-sickness, tears and loss of appetite which sig-
naled a famine when once recovered. My companions were very
kind to me but there came no rift in the clouds that had settled
o'er my spirits. We took a dreary walk through monotonous
streets where the houses were all brick and approached by flights
of white marble steps, and in dark nights when their numbers cannot be seen I am sure their occupants must be puzzled to find their
individual homes if no friendly street-lamp turns informant to the
belated citizen. I am thankful when the weary day is done, a day
so tedious to me yet to the citizens of New York City, remarkable
for the blowing up of Hell Gate and I was told that many of the
dwellers nearest the scene of the explosion, removed through
fear of its disastrous results. The explosion was under water and
raised a sheet of that fluid three acres in extent to the height of
fifty feet. Monday morning finds us on our way to the Exposition
grounds. We visit the Art Gallery also known as Memorial Hall,
a fire-proof building, costing $1,500,000, and designed to remain
as a permanent memorial of the nations' first Centennial Anniversary. The pictures were beyond my descriptive powers and I can
only say that I saw " Temptation, Adam and Eve in Paradise,"
" Samson and Delilah," " Prometheus bound, devoured by vult-
ures," " Eve with Cain and Abel." The statuary was lovely but

I must express my opinion upon both sculpture and painting as to the lack of drapery surrounding the characters represented. Ignorant country people, (if you so wish to designate them) having few advantages, are all the more acute to discern an impropriety if there be one, and this class of people not yet having had their native modesty blunted by familiar contact with the fashionable world who license naked picture painting, are shocked at beholding the human form on exhibition in so public a place, devoid of even the primitive clothing invented by Adam and Eve. These pictures are adorned (?) with all the reality of life, and come upon one's vision before he is aware of their proximity, and for a moment he is led to believe some poor lunatic has evaded the vigilance of her keepers and thrust herself before his eyes. If to be fashionable is to lay aside our decency, and, in a mixed crowd, such as thronged the Art Gallery, gaze unblushingly upon such artistic efforts, I for one would wish to be left to the obscurity of the country where in solitariness only the clear streams reflect the beauty of the innocent maiden. There was the statue of Bismark, costing four thousand dollars in gold,—the statue of the Daughter of Zion, lamenting over the ruins of Jerusalem, and the Youth of Michael Angelo. The entrance to this hall was grand with statuary. In the Annex was an oil painting of "Galileo before the tribunal of Spain." On leaving this building we call at the postoffice from which I extract two long letters, and the further pleasures of the day are gilded with the love-light of home reflected by so precious a talisman. While I rest on the easy couch in the elegant parlor of the Illinois State Building, and listen to the music of the piano, I muse that though I am surrounded by the *grandest* sight I ever expect to see, a *pleasanter* one is in prospective—a sight of husband and home. We next enter Machinery Hall, covering about fourteen acres and costing eight hundred thousand dollars. There were displayed the various sewing machines and their elegant stitching: a specimen of Cole's charmingly executed my name on a ground work of black cloth. Dummy's were arrayed in costumes comparing the difference in the styles of 1776 and 1876—the dress of the former century being a green satin under-skirt and light satin over-dress richly embroidered, and the latter time was represented by a figure in light pink satin. The basques to both costumes were similar, and pointed in front. There were dolls clothed in "purple and fine linen" of all sizes, and apparently of all ages. I noticed a mon-

5

strous propeller wheel and machines for printing—trains of cars
resting on rails of shining steel, and here in the center of the building was found the mammoth Corliss engine, the largest in the
world, of fourteen hundred horse power, capable of driving the
entire shafting necessary to run all the machinery exhibits.   In the
Annex was a tank one hundred and sixty feet long by sixty wide,
with a depth of ten feet. At the south end of this tank was a
water-fall thirty-five feet high by forty wide, supplied from the
tank by the pumps on exhibition. A small boat was moored on
the surface of the water. We saw the first printing press placed
in comparison with those in present use. Silk ties and suspenders
were being woven; pins manufactured and stuck at the rate of one
hundred and eighty thousand per day. Saw envelopes, brick and
shingles in process of formation, and a knitting machine operated
by turning a crank. It was knitting a stocking of red and black
yarn. We next visited the United States building, erected by the
United States Government at a cost of $60,000. It covers about
two acres. There we got on the war track and scouted inanimate
Sioux Chiefs—Red Cloud in indescribable paint and feathers—
Esquimaux—Indian idols—a Makah Indian, a female Indian skel-
eton or mummy— a wigwam—a miniature Patent Office—torpedo
boat guided by electricity, and boats of all descriptions—seamen of
the United States Navy—our own soldiers in blue, so lifelike yet
lifeless—furs worn by Dr. Kane in the Arctic region, also a bust of
the daring explorer—also soldiers with the uniform of the Continental infantry 1776—soldiers representing Morgan's rifles—a green
light-house—a whaling vessel—a lobster shell in full dress—wild
animals apparently ready to devour the intruder, but harmless as
kittens, in their inanimateness—sculls and endless curiosities of
Indian manufacture—a span of farm horses harnessed and ready for
the field, with mild eyes and marks of hard labor upon their
breasts—also saw the head of a whale from the Atlantic Ocean—a
musk ox—an Indian dug-out or canoe—a squaw's water-proof,
made of the intestines of the sea lion—also the largest pipe in the
world, costing two hundred and fifty dollars, and can not be dupli-
cated. I think it was made of ivory. It was coveted by every
masculine lover of the weed, no doubt. Next we marched into the
Kansas and Colorado building, which was ingeniously decorated
with grains. There was a bell constructed of cereals and designed
to imitate the old bell at Independence Hall. Grain strung upon

wire, hung in graceful festoons like some rare fringe. There was a very high pyramid of luscious apples—a white buffalo, stuffed—a case of birds killed and preserved by one woman's hand. Wild animals without life, stood upon a craggy mountain side and might well engage the attention of the hunter. A real, live rattle snake lent a charm to the scene. (The secret of the charm was, in its being securely enclosed in a box.) The Woman's Pavilion was next explored. It covers nearly an acre of ground, and cost thirty thousand dollars, paid by the voluntary contributions of the women of the United States. It is said to contain "everything women make that is worth showing." It did not quite meet my expectations, though the display was all fine, but it possessed no entirely new, striking feature, if we except perhaps, a patent dish-washer, which after carefully viewing, decided me to adhere to the old way. There was carpet weaving—a box containing turtles and bugs made of leather by Miss A. Williamson. The New England kitchen was designed to illustrate the New England kitchen of the present time as compared with that of one hundred years ago. It was made of logs and filled with old fashioned articles, and the lady attendants were in ancient dress. There were huge books scarcely legible with their queer "f's" in lieu of "s." Old spinning wheels that were the pride of the hearts of our grandmothers, also a folding chair, two hundred years old. The odor of baked beans and "Johnny cake" always drew a crowd in and around that building. Hop vines shaded the small windows and a few homely vegetables grew within a small enclosure, an apology for a garden. It required the constant care of a policeman to maintain quiet at the gateway of this humble cottage. Mr. and Mrs. B—— left the grounds at five o'clock to call on friends, and I felt quite homelike to be thus thrown on my own resources. I took the cars for a ride around the grounds. At that late hour but few were in them, and the view was splendid. The track being circular, one can see his own engine curving first to the right, then to the left. They seemed to manage to have the trains meet, when the train that I was on was going up grade, as it were, and the approaching engine had the appearance of colliding with that of our own, but we felt no shock and received no hurt. The sun was at that dreamy height that it seemed half wishful yet half sad to bid us good night. The neatly kept grounds wore their loveliest aspect, and the short green grass and blooming flowers and sparkling fountains and smooth lakes all seemed to be wooing a final glance from this day king, and shed their attractions as an enticement for his return, and strove to make this parting most regretful. When my ride was ended I sought the assistance of a policeman to see me safely on board the Girard Avenue car. Everything on wheels was packed full. I had to stand all the way home, but we were a jolly set. Indeed there was the utmost cordiality expressed between entire strangers during my whole journey, and all seemed honest people like myself. We were startled at seeing a span of horses attached to a barouche, running away, in Fairmount Park. I did not hear of the result, whether the coachman succeeded in getting the fiery steeds under his control, or whether more lives were sacrificed on the altar of pleasure. I reached the Park View Hotel which is not far from Girard College, at dark and passed the evening alone in my room, writing to the lonely ones at home, after listening to some very fair music executed by some parties from Beloit, Wisconsin. Young America was well represented in the person of a lad of some eighteen summers, I should judge. Praises were lavished upon him on every hand, and being the pet of his numerous friends, he was consequently in great danger of being spoiled. His voice, a perfect contralto, I could have better appreciated had it belonged to a miss of tender years, but believing in the "eternal fitness of things" I could not but think he was out of his sphere to thus usurp the province of the many young misses at his side, who seemed anxious to render their share of the vocal entertainment. They were well-bred little folks, and were having "such a lovely time" as they expressed it. Happy youth! devoid of care, with no thought of stocks and bonds and mortgages with interest due; but no doubt your fond parents take as much pleasure in anticipating your enjoyments as do you in participating in the pleasures *their* labor and forethought have provided the means to enjoy.

CHAPTER IX.

ON our arrival at the grounds Tuesday morning, September, 26th, we again visit the Main Building, and examine a bath-tub, worth two hundred dollars, lined with slate. A looking-glass costing one thousand dollars, with a frame of cut glass, though a beauty in itself, reflected the images of the passersby as nature made them, without lending any of its own charms to form or feature. In the Hawaiian department was lava, which when burn-ing, must certainly be beheld with consternation. There was a cloak made of the bark of the bread-fruit tree, trimmed with bells; a hat made of the arrow-root plant. In Japan was a bedstead worth twenty-five thousand dollars, made of small pieces of various kinds of wood, taking twenty persons five years to construct it. In Austria were slippers made of glass. There were two pieces of statuary being a representation of "hide and seek." It rained for two hours this day, and we reviewed the Main Building pretty thoroughly. We were over-taken by a dear friend, Mrs. D——, and another lady and her husband, from W——, our starting point. We visit the House of Public Comfort. Things were ex-tremely comfortable there for *cash*, but without a stuffed pocket-book one might as well seek comfort in cheaper quarters. I judged the country was prosperous, as that building always held a crowd who certainly paid for what they received, as I realized from exper-ience after purchasing one lunch there. The quality of the food was par excellent, but the quantity sent me away hungry after expending enough money for a substantial dinner at any first-class hotel. We took a survey of the foreign buildings and bazaar's, in the afternoon. I am inclined to be skeptical as to the genuineness of the Jerusalem trinkets, exposed to view by foreign looking per-sonages dressed in Oriental costumes, who might have been ordi-nary Jews, residents of our own country, for ought I know. The

Holy Land is a great distance from us, and not so easy of access as to justify the removal of such vast quantities of sacred wood, and relics, as were exhibited. This is an age of shams, but really if all those articles were genuine, Jerusalem must be pretty thoroughly stripped of its ornateness and remembrancers. We saw a Swedish school house, erected by workmen from Sweden, and all the materials were imported from that country. In the Annex to the Main Building, was Washington's traveling carriage in 1776, with four white horses attached, which were made of wood and painted white. We saw numbers of elegant vehicles of all shapes and designs, from the solemn hearse down to the jockey's sulky for horse racing purposes. In my rounds I saw a mummy, an Egyptian priestess or princess. Cremation is more conducive to post mortem beauty, than to be converted into a mummy, therefore I decide in favor of the urn and its ashes.

CHAPTER X.

O N the morning of the twenty-seventh, Mr. and Mrs. B—— left for New York. I arose at five o'clock A. M. for an early search after some remiss relation that left home the same day that I departed, and whom I had not seen since we left Washington. After riding three or four miles in the street cars I failed to discover their boarding place, and I alighted at the door of Mrs. D——'s stopping place, in time for breakfast. As I sat beside her husband at the table, he made the homely though trite remark that "chickens come home to roost." Truly I was as glad of their company a thousand miles from home and partook of their hospitality as freely as if I had been seated at their own board under their home roof, where I am ever welcome. There was a long table filled with W—— friends, among them our pastor, and we had a merry meal. We all repaired to the Centennial grounds for a day's further enjoyment. Just outside the grounds there was on exhibition, the wonderful "Siege of Paris;" which we proceeded to explore and were well satisfied with our investment of fifty cents, after becoming familiar with its mysteries narrated to us by a gentleman constantly in waiting, and who repeated the story every half hour. The picture of the siege was four hundred and eighty feet long and fifty-five feet high, and it was sixty-six feet from one stand point to the scene represented. It took thirty artists fifteen months to paint it. After depositing another half dollar at the self-registering turn-stile we were once more surrounded by the magic of the past. We enter Agricultural Hall, whose green roof covers ten and a quarter acres, at a cost of three hundred thousand dollars. There are fruits from all parts of the world, quantities of which were canned whole, and could not fail to tempt the poorest appetite. There was a pavilion made of cotton, and its pure white pillars resembled a mass of snow flakes, which the first glance of the sun might lay low. There was a span of splendid bay horses with shining harness, attached to a reaper with nothing factitious, unnatural to betray the handiwork of man. Horticultural Hall, constructed of stone, brick, glass and iron, has one and a half acres under cover, at a cost of three hundred thousand dollars. There we saw sugar cane from Havana, the Musk Dago or Sago, the largest plant in the hall—the date palm from Asia—the Talipot palm from Ceylon—an ornamental stand made of boquet-holders of satin in all colors—a stand of dried natural flowers—Terra-cotta works; in fact this building had an air of neatness, coolness and quiet that, to the visitors through the intensely hot season, must have been a very elysium. Here one might visit the tropics with impunity from wild beasts or embrace of the boa-constrictor; might sit under the shade of the palm without fear of its being up-rooted by the trunk of the elephant; but though the poisonous insect and its venomous sting were absent, one might not handle the delicate, tropical plants, nor so much as pluck one tiny leaf from their fragile stems. I separate from my companions at night and return to my hotel. I am assigned a smaller room, about the size of a clothes-press, but it appears clean and is cheerful with gas-light. Mrs. B—— has learned me to call for fresh bed-linen, and on an examination of the sheets, I find that this is a case that will warrant me in carrying out her instructions, and I ring for the chambermaid. A prompt compliance with my order puts me in possession of a pair of sheets, that in dampness could not be excelled. I call for hot water and warm up internally before trying their freshness. I have no encomiums for Fairmount water works on the Schuylkill river, from which Philadelphia receives its supply of water. To me the water is useless for drinking purposes, even after it is boiled. Some of the ladies told me they had never drank as much beer as they had quaffed since their arrival in the city, being driven to the intemperance by the bad water. The example is a bad one truly, but I am compelled by necessity to follow it, but trust my masculine acquaintances will not take my actions as a precedent from which to be guided.

CHAPTER XI.

THURSDAY, September 28th, is Pennsylvania's day at the Centennial, and having slept like a lark the previous night, the humid sheets notwithstanding, I am prepared for early rising and a further investigation of the whereabouts of my kinsmen, which search proves fruitless as before, and the street cars get so filled I am debarred from joining Mrs. D. and her party, as on the morning previous, and after a four miles circuit I reach the Centennial grounds, where already a vast crowd is congregated. I first seek the Woman's Pavilion, where, guarded by two policemen, is exhibited the "Butter Bust, by Mrs. Caroline S. Brooks, representing the dreaming Iolanthe, King Rene's daughter. This ingenious design set as a protoplast for her artistic sisters, was barren of bovine suggestions, and none but a modern scientist could have detected lactescence as the primordial in its creation. The day being made a national holiday, the grounds were early filled with processions of various orders, that of the Soldier's Orphan's, drawing tears to my eyes as I thought of the battle fields strewn with lifeless fathers who once held to their warm, loving hearts, these children that marched before me. The calliope whistled "Hold the fort," while the bells chimed the Marseilles hymn, and amid thrilling music the Governor of Pennsylvania was escorted to the State building, where he held his reception. The State buildings are in a row, some of them, especially Michigan, ornate with lattice work, and all present what is most prized by the tourist, a hospitable appearance. There is such a concourse of people (excelling in number any previous day) that it is utterly impossible to see anything inside the building, and the utmost efforts of the fuming police are powerless to protect the greensward from the tread of the invaders, intent on being the first to welcome the noted personages as under escort of the militia, headed by brass bands, they appear on the grounds. I pass the forenoon in wandering around, seeking some familiar face, but am rewarded only with the sight of the countenance of one of my neighbors in W———. Tired of all the pomp and display, I seat myself on the platform near one of the entrances to the Main building and take a last, retrospective gaze o'er the panorama that a week's stay has made familiar and dear to me. Unless my longevity equal that of our primeval ancestors, this must necessarily be my last centennial, and it was mete that I devote the closing moments in celebrating this my first and final centenary anniversary of our prosperous nation, to solemn thoughts born of recent communion with the strange, idealistic things of the past, and the realism of the present closely cemented by the tardy but certain elements of progression. British India, in Asia, overcoming the distance of eleven thousand five hundred and thirty-five miles, has offered her tribute to our glory and that of her own, in bringing rare products of the Torrid zone, to swell the mass of curiosities here congregated. Australia, the land of the convict, sends her wonders a distance of ten thousand two hundred and sixty miles, and places them at our command. Russia, exceeding all other countries in her extent of 7,227,870 square miles, excels in her display of costly silks and velvets and rich furs. China, with her exceeding population of 477,500,000 souls, has not been sparing of her grotesque manufactures which are so lavishly spread before our vision, we may almost estimate one article to each of her inhabitants. The Hawaiian Islands, with a minimum population of 62,959, are by no means in the back-ground with their exhibits of gorgeous plumage and articles of incomparable texture. Our own beloved United States, though but 3,634,797 square miles in extent, with a population of 45,316,000, requires the greatest number of square feet (189,234,) for the display of her wealth and grandeur.

which have been accumulating for a hundred years, and of which
there can be no diminution in the century that is but opening up
her infancy amid prosperity and peace with all nations. This Centennial Exhibition opened with imposing ceremonies, May 10th
1876, with an attendance of one hundred thousand people, the
President of the United States, his cabinet and other high officials,
together with Dom Pedro, Emperor of Brazil, and his Empress, being among the number. It closed, October 10th of the same year,
and the total cost is estimated at $8,500,000. Upon the toil and
trials incident to the perfecting of so grand a scheme, who shall
place an estimate? We were informed that the Main building had
sold for one million eight hundred thousand dollars. The amassing
of these treasures from the remotest ends of the inhabitable earth;
the preparing of a place suitable for their reception; the adorning
of the grounds with costly fountains and statuary; the grading of
seven miles of roads and foot-paths, and broidering them with red-
olant flowers; the constructing of bridges and summer-houses—all
this required abundant means, unsurpassed perseverance, Christian
patience and a master mind at the helm with efficient, obedient
subordinates ever ready to do his bidding. If there be one person
more than another who originated this nation's festivity of a half
year's duration, that has proven so successful, let his name be set in
our memories and cherished through the vista of coming ages. The
youngest in this generation cannot hope to be his successor. The
new born infant of to-day, perchance, a hundred years hence in the
decrepitude of old age, may hobble to a renewal of like splendors on
these very grounds; but the intellect to-day not yet developed to an
appreciation of *this* scene will *then* be too enfeebled to rightly estimate the value of the treasures of the next century's gathering, and
thus not possessing the vigor of ripe manhood will lose alike the
charm connected with the celebration of both eras. Farewell to
this people whose bodies terrestrial the coming years will convert
into dust, but whose souls will live on amid beauties celestial.
Farewell to the antiquities left for the admiration of a future generation. Farewell to all this perishable matter that must needs
change its form, not one particle of which can ever be irretrievably
lost. All this beauty will decay. The life of the fountains will be
sapped by the recondite workings of nature. The marble statue is
no less cold than will be the hand of the sculptor years hence. The
genius of the artist will have perished long ere the colors of his

pictures become dimmed by that great effacer—time; but the artist's
power though lost to earth, may be quickened by heavenly realities
that here were but imaginings. All the industrious hands that
have helped to rear these delicate structures of glass or raise the
solid walls of granite and iron, will one day lie idle awaiting their
future work appointed by their heavenly master. Blessed heaven
with its prepared mansions where each and every well-doer may
find a home. One last, lingering gaze and the Centennial gates
have closed upon me forever!

CHAPTER XII.

PHILADELPHIA, the largest city, as to area, in the United
States, and the second in population, lies between the Delaware and Schuylkill rivers, six miles above their junction and ninety-six miles from the Atlantic Ocean. It is twenty-two miles long
from north to south, with a breadth of five to eight miles. There
are over three hundred and fifty miles of paved streets, and more
buildings than any other city in the country. The city was founded
by William Penn, who came over from England in 1682, with a
colony of Quakers, and purchased the site from the Indians. The
first Congress assembled here, and the Declaration of Independence
was signed and issued here July 4th, 1776. The convention which
formed the Constitution of the Republic, assembled here in May
1787. Here resided the first President of the United States, and
here Congress continued to meet until 1787. The city was in possession of the British from September 1777 to June 1778, a result of
the unfortunate battles of Brandywine and Germantown. Its population in 1874, was 674,022. It is peculiarly rich in relics of its
early history. The oldest of these is the Old Swede's Church, which
was built in 1700. It is of brick, and still regularly used. In the
cemetery surrounding the church are grave stones dating from
1700. Penn's cottage, a little two-story brick house stands on

Letitia street, a few doors south of Market; it was built for Penn before his arrival in the settlement, and has withstood the march of improvement that has swept away so many more pretentious structures. Treaty monument, corner of Beach and Hanover streets, marks the site of the old elm tree under which Penn made his treaty with the Indians. The tree was blown down in 1810. Christ Church (Episcopal) contains the oldest chime of bells in America. Its steeple is one hundred and ninety-six feet high. Carpenter's Hall is a plain two-story brick building, where assembled the first Congress of the United Colonies. Hultzheimer's New House, where Jefferson penned the Declaration of Independence, is at the south-west corner of Market and 7th streets, and Franklin's grave is at the south-west corner of Arch and 5th streets. Number 239 Arch street, is noticeable as the place where the first American flag was made. Girard College was founded by Stephen Girard, a native of France, who died 1831. He bequeathed $2,000,000 for the purpose of erecting suitable buildings "for the gratuitous instruction and support of destitute orphans," and the institution is supported by the income of the residue of his estate, after the payment of certain legacies. On December 31st, 1874, the estate amounted to $6,104,862.22. The grounds embrace forty-two acres. In a room in the central or college building, known as "Girard's room," are preserved the books and personal effects of the founder. A statue of Girard stands at the foot of the stairway, underneath which he is buried." Permits to visit the college may be obtained by all classes of individuals, except clergymen, and why is that? Fairmount Park has an extent of nearly fourteen miles in length, being one of the largest in the world. Among other points of interest, they contain the Zoological gardens, with a fine assortment of American and European animals.

"Philadelphia boasts of more beautiful cemeteries than any other city in the country. The principal one is Laurel Hill, established in 1835, embracing two hundred acres, and its distinguishing feature is its unique garden, landscape, and the profusion of trees, shrubs and flowers which adorn it. Among the former, are some cedars of Lebanon, the first which bore fruit in the United States. Woodland cemetery contains the Drexel mausoleum, the finest in America. The United States Navy Yard, is located on the Delaware river, at the foot of Federal street, and encloses twelve acres. At one of the docks is the frigate Constitution, "Old Ironsides,"

the most renowned vessel of the American Navy. This yard will
be sold as soon as League Island is ready for occupancy. It is a
low tract of land of six hundred acres, at the confluence of the Delaware and Schuylkill rivers, and was presented by the city to the
United States Government, on condition of its being converted into
a great Naval depot." On leaving the Centennial grounds I took
the street cars for a ride about town. Visited Independence Hall,
which was so thronged with sight seers, but little could be seen,
and certainly nothing examined. I saw the old bell which was
first rung after the passage of the Declaration, but which will never
more ring out its clear tones for liberty. I stood in the east room
where met the Continental Congress, and on the fourth of July,
1776, adopted the Declaration of Independence which was publicly
proclaimed from the steps on the same day. I am told the room
presents the same appearance now as it did then. In Congress Hall
in the second story, Washington delivered his farewell address.
Independence Square, in the rear of Independence Hall, is inclosed
by a solid brick wall, and contains some majestic trees. It was
within this inclosure that the Declaration of Independence was first
publicly read, July 4th, 1776. Washington Square, diagonally
opposite, is celebrated for containing nearly every tree that will
grow in this climate, whether indigenous or not. As I rode along
the streets of this great city I saw many lovely homes, and no
doubt my interest would have been enhanced had I known the notoriety connected with them. While I was in a car drawn by one
horse, it was hailed by a black gentleman, i a suit of black broad-
cloth and a ruffled shirt front, with dazzling diamond embellish-
ments. He held in his arms a chubby baby, which presented an
aspect of snowy whiteness, with the exception of its round face and
dimpled fists. Its robes were rich with embroidery, and a filmy
lace cap hid but partially its curling wool. A few tightly twisted
locks escaped and covered its low, shining forehead. The wife and
mother was arrayed in rustling silk, with wide white ribbons dang-
ling a-la-mode from a gaudily arranged hat which set out her black
profile in alto-relievo. She held by the hand a bright little miss
of some four summers, with an opaque visage, the counterpart of
her mother's, and bits of muslin, laces and softest elve clothed her
cap-a-pie. Their delicate lace nose-blowers were heavily perfumed
with musk, and my partiality for that delightful perfume was then
and there completely destroyed. Evidently this was an aristocratic

off-shoot from one of the escaped F. F. V's. Though "fine feathers make fine birds," you can not make a beautiful white crow out of a black one. I am decided in my inherent skepticism on two points: first, as to any natural loveliness in the negro race, and secondly, as to there being beautiful Indian maidens born to the noble red men of the forest. Though I would not harm a hair of their heads, that the Great Spirit hath numbered, I must ever be a living prototype of Harriet Beecher Stowe's "Miss Ophelia," and gather my robes about me when approached by one of the enfranchised race. Near the Zoological Gardens I left the car, and walked along a narrow, quiet footpath, that I would not have believed existed in a city of Philadelphia's magnitude. I reached Girard Avenue bridge across the Schuylkill river, and what a scene met my gaze compared to the isolated nook I had but just explored. With the steam cars winding around the hill in the distance, with boats sailing on the navigable waters beneath my feet, with the street cars and vehicles crossing the bridge upon which I stood, and the park dotted with thousands of pedestrians, and barouches drawn by prancing steeds—surely every means for locomotion was spread before me, and I chose to exercise the perambulatory muscles of the human frame, that, guided by the will, I might pause a sufficient length of time to take in all the grandeur about me—yet, sometimes pressed by the crowd, I was borne along over the dangerous street crossings, or, perhaps absorbed in my wonderous gazing, I for a moment was forgetful of the hurrying throng and stood alone, supported by some friendly railing or convenient lamp-post. But I was among strangers, with the utmost freedom of feeling and action, and if any secretly adjudged me insane they would never take the trouble to incarcerate me in one of the many asylums, with which Philadelphia abounds. And thus I strode on till my room was gained, where I threw myself upon my couch to collect the confused mass of ideas which my afternoon's peregrination had awakened. Magnificent fire-works, surpassing all former empyreal displays, were announced for the evening's amusement, on the summit of George's Hill in Fairmount Park. Being disappointed in a masculine escort, I saw only a few rockets from the parlor window of the Park View House. But I am glad to escape the jam consequent on an attendance, and with a long, epistolary assurance from home that I am remembered and that though "distance may part us nothing can sever, hearts that like ours are united forever." I

seek early the land of dreams, and by so doing am rewarded with a
sound mind and rested body, on the morning of the 29th of September, which ushers in the day that is noted for my departure
from the home of the Quakers.

CHAPTER XIII.

I had an unintentional view of the city that morning, that I
was not in a frame of mind to appreciate. The baggage-man
at the hotel having checked my trunk to one depot and directed
me to another, necessitated my waiting at what is called the Centennial Depot, for a period of about three hours, expecting momentarily the arrival of my baggage. After the departure of three
trains for New York City I could endure the delay no longer and
mounted on the seat of an Express wagon, (whose altitude was
not to my liking and the vehicle too unpretentious by far), I was
conveyed back to the hotel where I interviewed the proprietor in as
strong terms as became a lady tourist. I made known my wants
which were in effect that a horse and carriage be placed at my
command instanter and an immediate search for that trunk insti-
tuted—, that it could not of its own volition take itself out of the
city and if it were yet within the radius of the one hundred and
twenty-four square miles of Philadelphia I proposed to recover it.
A poor horse that hadn't been permitted to seek his quarters till
three o'clock in the morning, (being on duty all the previous night,
conveying its share of the dense throng that witnessed the fire
works, back to the city), dragged a sickly looking light wagon
before the door, with an oil-cloth top insufficient to protect ought
but the seat, the capacious rear being intended for the storing of
baggage. Into this carry-all I disposed myself, seated beside a
sleepy looking youth who had shared the last night's vigils of this
"heavey" old horse, and to whom nature in the beginning of the
boy's creation, had allotted two eyes, but one having become im-
paired by stress of vision or other accident, he had altogether the

appearance of a one-sided, down-trodden, oppressed individual, and judging from his physiognomy I was by no means satisfied that his principles and habits were of the first order. He was not much given to loquacity and divided his time between urging the horse with the reins and gazing into nothingness with his blind eye. The result of this anxious ride was favorable and I embraced the receptacle of my treasures, found safely housed in the Pennsylvania Depot, among piles on piles of other baggage. I dismissed my servant of the hour with good wishes accompanied by a piece of silver. The Pennsylvania Depot is a large, fine building and held a crowd waiting for transportation by rail to New York City. It must have been between two and three o'clock, P. M. when the announcement came that our train was ready for occupancy. The few moments passed in waiting for this mass of humanity to file through the straight and narrow gate, were filled with well grounded fears of pick-pockets and I held tightly to my valuables and had it not been for the encircling arm of a veteran policeman who gently pushed me through the passage while I held my ticket up for inspection, I think I should have been left standing there to this day, a monument of stupefaction. Gracefulness was unthought of and all ran as fast as their limbs and loads would allow. The cars filled rapidly and I was only just in time to secure the last seat near the stove, which I shared with a polished French gentleman, a resident of New York City, but his accent was so broken, much of the information he kindly volunteered me along the route, was entirely lost. The train, of some twenty cars, was run in sections and I was tormented with fears whether it would be our destiny to dash into the train ahead of us or be smashed by the oncoming one. The fates had no such calamity in store for us. The Pennsylvania Railroad encircles the Centennial grounds and we had a view of the tops of the buildings as we started on our journey. The train halted at the Centennial Depot where my morning had been passed in fruitless watching, which had it been avoided would have enabled me to have reached New York by ten o'clock A. M. As it was it would be near nightfall before I could possibly reach the friends awaiting my coming. It is a delightful ride from Philadelphia to New York City, a distance of ninety miles which it takes three hours to overcome. The land in New Jersey is low and swarms with gallinippers. Thirty-two miles from Philadelphia we reach Trenton where we

cross the Delaware river. Here Washington won his famous
victory over the Hessians, December 26th 1776. Newark, New
Jersey, nine miles from New York City, contains one hundred thousand inhabitants. The Highlands of New Jersey are pointed out
to me. On reaching Jersey City, I concluded it must be consid-
erable of a place, as the cars were being emptied of their live freight
very rapidly, and among them my French companion. As he arose
to leave, it struck my mind that perhaps I ought to follow the
crowd, and I asked him if that was the place for me to alight. He
said it was, and the manner in which I hustled my traps together
would be an advanced lesson for snails to take in the rudiments of
speediness. I was in the predicament of "my son John" in the
nursery rhyme, who had "one boot off and one boot on," neverthe-
less I landed on the platform, *in toto*, and though not a specimen of
tidiness, I was at least presentable, and kept my eye on the white
hat of the Frenchman, lest I be led to the wrong ferry. My ideas
of a ferry were rather confused, and extremely crude. I had never
seen but one ferry boat, and that resembled a raft, and skum over
the river amid the creaking and grinding of a rusty old chain on
pulley's. I knew where there was a ferry there was water, but not
a drop was in sight. I noticed the passengers one by one dart
through a narrow opening where a fat man stood at a little window
and as they passed they gave him money, which he accepted without thanks. He only asked me for two cents, which I gave him
for charity's sake, and wondered what misfortune he had met with
to be dependent on the public generosity. His corpulency suggested a bloated bond holder come to grief, and I half wished I had my
pennies back. While these thoughts were flying through my mind
I had been following the throng, that rushed pell-mell for what
seemed to me like a covered bridge open only at one end. Horses
and wagons stood in the center of the supposed bridge, and people
walked along at the sides and were lost to my view. Presently
bridge, people, horses and all moved off, and I saw water beaten
to a foam by some marine monster, but its calmness was soon re-
gained, and I was initiated into the mysteries of a first-class ferry,
and while I stood watching the performance I was made to understand that I had missed the boat, and would be obliged to wait five
minutes for another. I stepped into the waiting room, and when
the next boat touched the wharf I boarded it with as much pomposity as I could summons on a short notice, and walking to the

7

front I took a seat with the coolness of an Atlantic whaler setting
out on his first sea voyage. Our boat getting in the track of a
large steamer, gave a few undulatory motions that threatened an
upheaval of my scanty breakfast of coffee and doughnuts at the
Centennial depot, but a few vigorous swallows turned the tide, and
I recovered my equanimity. Safely across the Hudson river, I took
a horse-car through New York till I reached East river, where I
encountered another ferry boat which landed me at Brooklyn. A
short ride on the street cars, and I am tremblingly standing at the
door of No. 47, Rush Street, Brooklyn, E. D. as per directions. My
ring at the door-bell is answered, and a voice disturbing an echo of
my childhood says, "come right in, I know you." What a welcome these words contained, and I did not hesitate to partake of
the hospitality they offered. It had been twenty years since I had
seen the faces of the dwellers in this elegant abode. Loving me
when but a *child*, they now greeted the *woman*, as though there had
been no intervention of long, eventful years. I was nearly overcome with the days anxiety and exciting travels and a motherly
hand removed the bonnet of which I was forgetful, and that I had
worn since the early morning. I broke the day's fast by partaking
of a hearty supper, and retired early, the sound of the merriment
coming up from below disturbing me not, but rather wooed me to
the sweet slumber which I indulged in till a late hour the following
morning.

CHAPTER XIV.

SATURDAY, my first day in Brooklyn, was dark and rainy without, but within doors, a cheerful fire in the grate and lively conversation with my hostess and family, dispelled all dreariness. I was suffering much with a cold in my head, but despite clouds and sneezing I was very happy in this retired, city home. Sunday, October 1st, was a bright, glorious Sabbath, and I open my trunk for the first time since it was packed at home, and donning my best garments, we journeyed a distance of three miles on the street cars, to the renowned Plymouth Church, presided over by Rev. Henry Ward Beecher. Our party were fortunate in being offered a seat by a kind, elderly gentleman, the acceptance of which commanded for us a full view of the minister, choir and a closely packed congregation. Hundreds went away without even as much as a peep into the vestibule, for the church literally overflowed with curious humanity anxious to hear this, the noted divine's first sermon since the close of his summer vacation. I doubt not that there were daring ones among the waiting crowd that would have clung to the church spire if by so doing they were enabled to hear the utterances of this man whose notoriety is universal. There was nothing particularly striking about the discourse. There was an eloquent allusion to the twittering birds that so fill the green boughs of the trees, in the seclusion of the country—the same feathered songsters that sang in the heart of that little, lone woman as she dusted "father's" chair ready for his reception when he "dropped in" of a morning for a frolic with Theo's rollicking children. The long, gray locks of this afflicted pastor were none too smoothly brushed; he wore no shining suit of broad cloth with the elements of newness about it, but plain and unvarnished, he stood before us with an unfaltering faith in the gospel, that religious barque that had battled with the assailants of his reputation, and upon whose

banners waving at the mast-head, he hoped to inscribe—victory!
I saw an aged, sorrow stricken form in a seat near the front; her
silver hair was smoothly brushed away from her wrinkled brow; her
sweet face bore the impress of christian forbearance and wifely for-
giveness, and innocence sat enthroned in every lineament. She
was the wife of Henry Ward Beecher. A poor looking old man,
who wore a skull-cap, presided at the organ, and the choir of sixty
or more, at the close of the sermon, continued to worship the God
of our fathers in grand anthems whose melody filled my soul. By
the discourse I had failed to be lifted up, but the music was such as
hath power to "calm the savage breast to peace." In the afternoon
I was escorted to Prospect Park, containing five hundred and fifty
acres. Huge, old trees contribute to its shade, and cooling rills
take one in imagination to the depths of the country. It contains
eight miles of drives. The lake covers sixty-one acres. We pass
the Sabbath evening at home in pleasant conversation.

CHAPTER XV.

MONDAY morning, October 2d, we repair to New York City
for a view of Central Park, one of the largest and finest in
the world, containing eight hundred and forty-three acres, entered
at eighteen different points. It is crossed by four streets, to afford
opportunity for traffic which pass under the park and drives. Between 79th and 96th streets are two Croton reservoirs, one compris-
ing thirty-five and the other one hundred and seven acres. The
five lakes occupy forty-three and one-half acres. There are ten
miles of carriage roads and thirty miles of foot paths. The Mall
near the fifth Avenue entrance, is the principal promenade, shaded
by elm trees in double rows. We were disappointed at not hearing
the band in the Music Pavilion. At the termination of the Mall is
the Terrace, a lofty pile of masonry richly carved. We descended
the Terrace by a flight of broad stone steps, and beheld Central

Lake with its waters sparkling in the sunlight, and fragile boats dancing on the surface. Between the Terrace and the Lake we saw a fountain whose cost is said to excel any on the continent. There is a colossal statue of the Angel of Bethesda. We entered the American Museum of Natural History, which occupies the old State Arsenal. We saw savage animals, and birds without number, with the most lovely plumage. Monkeys chattered and performed various antics for our amusement, and a huge seal screeched and floundered in a tank constructed for its use. Animals with strange humps and horns, grazed in an enclosure, and altogether our stay at the Park was most delightful. In a tour of the city we pass Bellevue hospital, the largest in the city, accommodating one thousand two hundred patients. Blackwells Island, one hundred and twenty acres in extent, is pointed out to me as containing the prison where Tweed was confined. We pass the Tombs, a gloomy looking structure indeed. We also pass a building commenced by Tweed, but unfinished, and now under its ruins live disreputable characters. By this time it is mid-day, and we have reached the house occupied by an old school-mate of mine, whose birth-day would have been coeval with mine, had it occurred a week sooner. I remember him only, as a handsome, curly-headed boy, whose juvenile attentions were much sought after, and I was unprepared for the sight of a stalwart man with banking responsibilities upon his shoulders, the husband of a dear little woman and the father of a bright-eyed boy, with shining curls, and the sweetest of smiles and rosiest of cheeks and lips. After partaking of their hospitality for a short hour, we visit Stewart's store, constructed of iron painted white, and five stories high. No sign or placard advertise the elegance within, or mar the beauty of the plain exterior. Its interior presents an aspect of neatness, and order and richness is displayed on every hand. We mingle in the Babel of confusion on Broadway, and note its unsurpassed splendor without envy. We take a look at Washington Square, containing eight acres, and Steinway's piano rooms, and other places of interest that I shall note in summing up my description of this wonderful city. We arrive at Brooklyn, fatigued in mind and body, but I am not so exhausted but what I do full justice to the bountiful supply of edibles spread for our epicurean enjoyment. To me, there is no comparison in the goodness between the substantial food found upon the tables of private families and served by familiar, cleanly hands, and that obtained at the common run of public houses, prepared in dirty kitchens and dished up by black servants, who in all proba- bility have scratched their wooly heads preparatory to mixing the biscuit, or as a seasoning process, slapped their colored brother in the face with the beef-steak before placing it over the coals.

CHAPTER XVI.

THE six o'clock meal dispatched, we decide to return to New York City, and attend the concert given at Gilmore's Gar- den that evening. Those of my readers who have ever indulged in the youthful sport of playing in "Gideon's band," where each jolly juvenile is allotted a chimerical instrument upon which he is sup- posed to execute, in pantomime, the most difficult airs, quite inde- pendent of his neighbors melody, (which is in operation at the same time) but which instrument they must immediately relinquish, and mimic their leader as he in turn plays on the different imaginary instruments, and woe be to the neoterical musician if he does not follow the movements of the master,—with this experience before you, you can form an idea of how I was affected by Gilmore's Grand Orchestra, each member of which blew enough wind through their brass horns to raise any roof less firmly riveted than the one cover- ing the Concert Garden. The *noise* was a success; the *melody* a failure; that is, from where I sat, and my proximate companions agreed with me. Personally, Gilmore is grand and stately, and no doubt master of all he undertakes. He certainly had those ladies and gentleman under the perfect control of the stick he flourished in his gloved hand, and the bright buttons on his military uniform, flashed in the gas light with all the brilliancy of a purer metal. The vocal part of the performance was either beyond my appreciation or else it did not amount to much, and I am inclined to the latter statement, for I consider myself a judge of such common songs as the "Star Spangled Banner," but on an attempted rendition of that national air by Madame Somebody, I was puzzled to know whether the old flag still waved in the good old fashioned way or whether the terrific *squall* then prevailing had not torn our emblem of freedom in tatters. Women are taking great liberties with the rights of men now-a-days, but when a full brass band, composed of long-winded Germans, gets ready to play, I think it is time for a woman to wind up her trills; but this Madam kept right on amid the din of wind instruments as if her voice was being accompanied by the dulcet tones of harp or guitar instead of the deafening roar of a hurricane. And how she did scream in falsetto tones that would have burst the bonnet-strings of any modest maiden, member of a village church choir. The cornet solos executed by Mr. M. Arbuckle and Mr. J. Levy, were the only acts I could heartily applaud, and their musical talents are certainly unequaled in this or foreign climes. The "Garden" was decorated with blooming flowers, and ornamented with statuary and rustic seats, and near the entrance was a cavern adown whose rocky sides water trickled melodiously. The scene was lit by colored gas light, resembling round balls, and placed equidistant in semi-circles over our heads. But all the beauty was marred by stifling tobacco smoke and incessant beer drinking. I was glad to escape the fumes and breathe again the pure out-door air, if one can call air pure that is constantly being appropriated by such a conglomerate mass of humanity as is sheltered under the municipal law of the Empire City. I again meet my W—— acquaintances, and find they have as much comprehensiveness of the musical performance as myself. We cross the ferry by moonlight, and standing on the deck of the boat, the Great All Seeing Eye seemed to have singled us out and beamed upon us with loving watchfulness and benignity. I could imagine no crime committed on such an effulgent night. The heavens spake too plainly of the glory of the All Father, and the vigilance of the angels must be of avail under the radiance of this lunar and stellar light.

CHAPTER XVII.

TUESDAY morning, October 3d, I bid adieu to my Brooklyn friends, and meeting Mrs. D. at the ferry, we took first the horse cars then the steam cars for Coney Island. On our arrival there we meandered the sandy beach and inhaled the fresh sea breezes and shuddered the while at the wreck and ruin these daring waves might cause, did we permit a freedom of their caresses. We gathered the soft, white sand and sea-shells, and then sat down to listen to the ever murmuring sea. The billows of the Atlantic wafted no tales to our receptive ears. We watched a sail recede from view with grateful feelings that we were on solid terra-firma. The next point of interest was Greenwood cemetery, said to be the most beautiful in the world, and containing four hundred and thirteen acres. Since 1842, one hundred and seventy-eight thousand interments have been made. The main entrance is one hundred and thirty-two feet long and forty feet deep, the pinnacle in the center being one hundred and six feet high. It is sculptured with scenes from the bible, the main ones being the entombment and resurrection of Christ. The grounds have seventeen miles of carriage roads and fifteen miles of footpaths. The soldiers monument on a raise of ground, presents a view of the two cities, and their surrounding waters. The sun shone warmly down upon the green sodded roofs under which slept the inhabitants of this silent necropolis, but alas its revivifying rays were lost, for, if we believe the scriptures, not till the dread Judgment Day when the last trump shall sound, shall these bodies be quickened and arise and depart to the right or left, as the Omnipotent hand may dictate. The costly, imposing monument spoke not more plainly of a remembrance of the dear departed, than did the toys and homely tokens of love arranged in glass cases and placed o'er the graves of the little darlings recalled to heaven. The toil and worry in the busy, bustling world, will never cease to add new inmates to these subterranean homes. The work was still going on, and a heap of moist, fresh earth, marked the place where an open grave was waiting for the interment of some soulless body. But for such deep gulfs of despair in the pathway of life, many a journey through this world would be made in gaiety and worldliness, with never an uplook toward heaven or a thought of the eternal. While we resume our long street-car ride and bid adieu to Brooklyn, perhaps for ever, I will detail a few of its most interesting points not yet mentioned. It is the third largest city in the United States, separated from New York by the East river, and is at the west end of Long Island. From north to south it is seven and three-fourths miles long, and its average breadth is three and one-half miles. It was settled in 1625. On the Heights back of the city the battle of Long Island was fought August 26th 1776, and the Americans were defeated with a loss of two-fifths of their men engaged. Its population in 1870 was 396,099. It has few hotels, but many fine boulevard's, and is known as the "City of Churches." R. S. Storrs is the pastor of the Church of the Pilgrims, and Talmage's Tabernacle is said to be the largest Protestant Church in America. The United States Navy Yard covers forty-five acres of ground. The Dry Dock is said to be one of the most remarkable structures of the kind in the world, is built of granite and cost $2,113,173. It holds 610,000 gallons of water and can be emptied by steam pumps in four and one-half hours. The Atlantic Dock has an area of forty-two and one-half acres, and water of sufficient depth to accommodate the largest ships. The wharfage is two miles in extent. "The piers are of solid granite, and surrounding the basin on all sides, except an entrance two hundred feet wide for vessels, are substantial brick, and granite warehouses. In crossing Fulton ferry to or from New York the massive towers of the bridge are conspicuous objects. Their height above high water is two hundred and sixty-eight feet. The bridge itself when completed will be six thousand feet long, and the span across the river from tower to tower one thousand five hundred and ninety-five feet long. It will be eighty-five feet wide including a promenade of thirteen feet, two railroad tracks and four wagon or horse car tracks. From high water mark to the floor of the bridge in the center, will be a distance of one hundred and thirty-five feet, so that navigation will not be impeded. The approach on the Brooklyn side from the terminus to the anchorage,

8

will measure eight hundred and thirty-six feet; on the New York side, one thousand three hundred and thirty-six feet. Its cost will be about $10,000,000." We reach Broadway, New York, in the middle of the afternoon and perambulate till evening this great central thoroughfare of the city eighty feet wide, and stopping at some of the mammoth retail stores, we make a few purchases, there by familiarizing ourselves with the manners and customs of the elite of the city while they are out on their shopping expiditions, sending in their orders for some such trifle as a bit of lace, or diamond pin, the bill for which amounts to hundreds of dollars, but the cost is immaterial to those favored votaries of fashion rolling in their wealth, yet often lacking two of the most desirable elements of life—health and happiness. Weak and faint with the days travels and fast, the six o'clock dinner-bell at Mrs. D.'s boarding house, where we were stopping, was a pleasant sound to hear, and I quite forgot good, old Dr. Hall's admonitions about hearty evening meals, as the variety of viands was placed before me in pursuance to my orders. After a half hours pleasant converse in the parlor, we repaired to our rooms seeking the repose we so much needed. Before my eyes danced alternately the gay and solemn splendors that had made of the day a brief dream. The tinkling car-bell and rumbling wheels on the pavements reverberated in my ears. One moment I was rejoicing with those who rejoiced, the next, mourning with those who mourned. Now, standing on some dizzy pinnacle taking a bird's eye view of land and water below, again, I was tossed by the ocean's billows, or floating idly down some limped stream. Women, attired in costly velvets and dazzling diamonds, led by the hand ragged urchins and decrepit old men. Horses with heads like lions and tails of serpents, were gaily caparisoned and attached to elegant barouches, whose inmates were the resurrected from the mausoleums of Greenwood, in long, white robes and starry crowns upon their foreheads, emblazoned with the warning words, "Tis better to go to the house of mourning than to the house of feasting."

CHAPTER XVIII.

AMONG the geographical and historical accounts of the city of New York, none are so explicit as the description of that renowned city, found in the "Hand-Book of American Cities," and the author of that valuable work will pardon me if I cull from its pages much useful information, arrogating nothing to myself but giving the praise to him, to whom it is justly due. "This great commercial metropolis of the United States, and largest city of the western Hemisphere, is situated at the mouth of the Hudson river on New York Bay. It covers the entire surface of Manhattan Island, as well as numerous other islands in the East river. Its extreme length north from the Battery, is sixteen miles. Its greatest width from the Hudson to the Bronx river, is four and one-half miles. It covers twenty-six thousand five hundred acres, of which twelve thousand acres are on the mainland. Manhattan Island, on which the city proper stands is three and one-half miles long, and varies in breadth from a few hundred yards, to two and one-fourth miles—having an era of fourteen thousand acres, to which the islands in the East river add four hundred more. The harbor of New York is one of the finest and most picturesque in the world. (Perhaps the time is not far distant when its rival will be that of San Diego, California, whose praises are already being bruited by officious reporters and anxious railroad officials.) The outer bar of New York harbor is at Sandy Hook, eighteen miles from the Battery. Hendrick Hudson, an Englishman, in the service of the Dutch East India Company arrived at the site of the present city, September 3d, 1609. He afterwards ascended the river as far as the site of Albany, and claimed the land by right of discovery, as an appendage of Holland. In 1614 a Dutch colony came over and began a settlement. In 1664 it was surrendered to the British, and passing into the hands of the Duke of York, was called New York. In 1696 Trinity Church was founded. In 1711 a slave market was established in Wall street. The American army under Washington occupied the city in 1776, but after the battles of Long Island and Harlem Heights, it was captured by the British forces and remained their headquarters for seven years. The British troops evacuated the city November 25th 1783. The Erie canal was completed in 1825. It is estimated that there are one million five hundred thousand persons in New York at noon on every secular day. Delmonico's restaurant, at the corner of 5th Avenue and 14th street, is one of the best dining places in the world, and is famous for its elaborate dinners. The Grand Central Depot, in 42d street, between 4th and Madison Avenue, is the largest and finest in the country; it cost nearly $2,250,000. It is six hundred and ninety-two feet long and two hundred and forty feet wide, and admits one hundred and fifty cars. The depot of the Pennsylvania railroad is reached by ferries, from foot of Desbrosses and Courtland streets. The elevated railway runs from the Battery to Central Park, at 59th street. The track is supported by iron pillars and the cars are luxurious, and drawn by small locomotives. Wall street, less than a half mile long, running from Broadway opposite Trinity Church to the East river, is the monetary centre of the country. It contains the custom-house and United States sub-treasury. Fifth Avenue is the favorite promenade, and almost exclusively devoted to private residences. Castle Garden, on the sea-verge of the Battery, was built in 1807 as a fortress, (Castle Clinton.) It was ceded to the city in 1823, and was the scene of the civic receptions of the Marquis de Lafayette, Gen. Jackson, President Tyler and others. Subsequently it became an opera house, and here Jenny Lind, Sontag and Mario made their appearance. The building is now used as a depot for immigrants, and the chief receiving and distributing reservoir of the great tide of immigration from Europe. Bowling Green, the cradle of New York, is just north of the Battery; in the times of the Dutch it was the court end of town, and surrounded by the best houses. The Kennedy House, No. 1, Broadway, was built in 1760, and is one of the most interesting relics now left standing. In colonial times it was the heart of the fashion in the colony, having been secessfully the residence and headquarters of Lords Cornwallis and Howe, Gen. (Sir Henry) Clinton and Gen. Washington. Talleyrand also lived there during his stay in this country. Arnold occupied No. 5, Broadway, and in Clinton's headquarters his treasonable projects were concerted. Fulton died in 1815 in a room in the present Washington Hotel. Washington's farewell interview with the officers, took place at France's tavern, corner of Pearl and Broad streets, long since removed. The new postoffice cost between six and seven million dollars, and was occupied in '75. The new Court House, occupied since 1867, but not yet completed, has walls of white marble; the beams and stair cases are of iron. The cost of the building and furniture was over $12,000,000; the result of the notorious "Ring frauds" of which it was the instrument. The United States sub-treasury is a white marble building at the corner of Wall and Nassau streets. Formerly the old Federal Hall stood on this site, and the spot is as classic as that whereon Washington delivered his inaugural address. The new Tribune building is the loftiest on the island, and the largest and best appointed newspaper office in the world, and is absolutely fire-proof. A. T. Stewart's marble building, devoted to wholesale trade, stands on the site of one of the principal forts erected by the British for the defense of the city during the Revolution. Stewart's palace, as it is called, on the corner of 5th Avenue and 34th street, is the finest private residence in America. It is of white marble, three stories high, besides the basement and mansard roof, and cost $3,000,000. A fine gallery of paintings is one of its chief attractions. Manhattan market, at the foot of 34th street, North river, is one of the largest structures of the kind in the world, and adjoining it is a plaza, capable of accommodating five hundred wagons. The National Academy of design, corner of 4th Avenue and 23d street, is a unique building of gray and white marble and blue stone. The plan of the exterior was copied from a famous palace in Venice. There are about three hundred and seventy churches of all denominations in the city. Trinity Church (Episcopal) has the finest chime of bells in America. In the grave-yard surrounding the church are the tombs of Alexander Hamilton, Robert Fulton and Charlotte Temple. The yard covers nearly two acres of ground. Dr. Tyng presides over St. George's (Episcopal) Church, one of the largest in the city. The Church of the Transfiguration (Episcopal) is known as "the little church around the corner," and is noted for its half rustic, picturesque character. Dr. Chapin presides over the Divine Paternity (Universalist). The largest church edifice in the city, and one of the largest and finest on the continent is St. Patrick's Cathedral, in 5th Avenue, and but half finished. There are upward of

four hundred schools and institutions of learning in the city, and
two hundred and thirty-nine charitable institutions. Cooper Insti-
tute founded and endowed by Peter Cooper, has three thousand
students in all departments. Opposite is the Bible House, the property of the American Bible Society, next to the British, the largest
in the world, and here all the operations of that important organi-
zation are carried on. The Five Points House of Industry and Five
Points Mission face each other on what was once the vilest and
most dangerous part of the city. The Battery at the south extrem-
ity of the city, looking out on the Bay embraces twenty-one acres.
Hell Gate, long the terror of vessels entering or leaving the harbor
by way of Long Island Sound, is a collection of rocks in the channel which offering much resistance to the tides causes a succession
of whirlpools and rapids." This dangerous place was the scene of
the great explosion before mentioned, which took place Sunday
September 24th 1876. Much hard labor yet remains to be performed before the rocky barriers entirely disappear. Thus endeth
our tour of New York City, guided by the friendly hand of "D.
Appleton, & Co.," whose handsome publishing house stands in the
vicinity of the St. Nicholas and Metropolitan Hotels. But for the
useful knowledge gained from the descriptive volumes issuing from
that great house, I should long since have become bewildered in
some of the narrow, mixed up streets of the city, or hopelessly
stranded on the ocean of its grandeur.

CHAPTER XIX.

EDNESDAY morning October fourth, burst upon us in truly oriental splendor and ere the fifth matutinal hour was reached, my garments were arranged with reference to the day's duties and pleasures, the first of which was the pursuit of my second self during this trip, namely,—my trunk. It had been checked from Brooklyn to some pier from which the day-boat from New York city to Albany plied the Hudson, but *which* pier had been the momentous question of the waking hours of the previous night, and my morning thoughts were agitated to that pitch that even the enticements of a downy bed and early dreams "sure to come true," had not the power to woo me. Leaving the sharer of my couch, the partner of my joys and sorrows *pro tem*, our dear sister Doyle, to indulge in the luxury the center of a warm bed is sure to produce, I set forth for the pier nearest our boarding place, some dozen blocks distant, making frequent inquiries of policemen to assure myself I was facing the right direction, and then I went ahead in true Westonian style.

On reaching my destination I found the baggage master was yet in the land of dreams and all was silent as a deserted fort, deserted save one sentinel, who guarded what I supposed to be the little Leviathan chained to this pier, but which afterward proved to be the steamer "Armenia," that was destined to rock us on the bosom of the Hudson for miles northward, but vain were its wooings, and, dreamy as were the sounds of the rippling waves our eyes could not close and shut out God's master-piece of creation—the banks of the Hudson. But I must not leave that sentinel standing guard so long, not with gun in hand, but a wooden bucket which he now and then lowered to the water—filled and dashed on the head of this animal, this huge Leviathan that sat on the face of the waters so triumphantly. I ventured an inquiry as to where I might find the person in charge of the baggage stowed at that point. The gallant marine leaped from the back of the animal and soon aroused from slumber the tardy baggage master. But THE trunk to me of all trunks, was not there, and I turned my back on that wharf determined to lose no time in reaching Thirty-ninth pier, one and a half miles distant. "That Brooklyn express-man must have the absent-mindedness of a Beecher who mistook Tilton's house for his own," I said to myself as I indignantly hailed a street-car. The track ran parallel with the river, and casting my eyes over the inmates of the crowded car, visions of all I had heard and read of river rats, kidnappers, thieves and murderers, arose in my mind and I was right in their midst judging from a *prima facia* view of the case. Even the Grab-man of Watseka, might be there disguised in the garb of a *day* laborer in lieu of his nocturnal uniform, and at an opportune moment might confront me with denunciatory words as the cause of his exile from his native western wilds. If there was one more dirty and whose filth excelled in its age, it was he who offered me a seat. I took his place, however, squeezed in between two men whose visages suggested the veritable Charley Ross captors. There was one female aboard and though she was of foreign extraction, shabby and evidently destitute of the cardinal graces, I was thank-ful for her presence and could well exclaim with brother Russell, "God bless the women!" For a weary half hour did that car drag at a snail's pace past dens of perdition that bordered the track on either side. I caught frequent views of the river lying so peaceful in the morning sunlight and wondered why God did not cause its waters to rise in a body and sweep from the earth such wretched-ness as o'ershadowed its banks. Ten thousand times ten thousand fathoms of the Hudson would it take to cleanse this footstool of its sin and iniquity; thus the waters are left for man to utilize in the transportation of freight, animate and inanimate, from north to south, from east to west. Thirty-ninth pier was reached at last and a polished mulatto, polished in manners and complexion, answered my questions as to where I would be most likely to find my trunk. The muscles that had gradually strengthened during my centennial trip, did not fail me now as I ran with what speed my trailing skirts would allow, past doors leading I cared not whither, for, like a hound that has caught its first sight of the game it is pursuing, had

I a glimpse of the treasure of my soul—the casket containing the *all* of womankind—her best clothes. I could not be mistaken. Almost within my grasp rolled a truck, guided by the hand of some stout foreigner, who perhaps carried in his pocket his precious naturalization papers of recent date, the effect of the importunities of some disciple of Tilden and Hendricks, who had secured him for his vote for the presidential election, the result of which is yet in the dim distance. But that trunk. It was not of the Flora McFlimsy order, but a modest unpretentious looking affair, well secured by half of the home clothes line, which, hitherto tenaciously guarded, had been ruptured for this sacred purpose. Over the clothes line was bound a broad, new leathern strap, and altogether to an observing mind that trunk had the appearance of perfect security. If those things *did* give out, it would be a clear case of the perversity of inanimate nature. Do you ask did I know that trunk? Know it? Was I not instinctively guided to it among the confusion of baggage in that babel city of brotherly love, Philadelphia? Every jam and bruise on that trunk were like so many incisions in my proud flesh. Well, I caught that supposed voter of the Tilden ticket and told him where that precious baggage was destined. He pledged me his word (and who doubts a democrat's word?) that it would be safely consigned to the steamer "Daniel Drew," consequently, would be drawn to Albany in due time. I returned the way I had come, rejoicing. What little jewelry I possessed I kept carefully concealed under my cloak, and landing safely at the corner of West Fourteenth street, I soon found the number from whence I had started some two hours before. But what was my consternation on finding our beloved sister Doyle, usually so wide awake on society nights, still slumbering, peacefully without a sigh or a snore. "Only three-quarters of an hour for breakfast and the pier!" I shouted, and, there was running in hot haste and mustering of super-human strength in the arraying of humanity for the day's battle.

With me, breakfast is something that will not bear abridgment, and one-half of that three-quarters of an hour I passed in communion with the waiters of that establishment, the beefsteak and hot biscuit, eschewing the half ripe tomatoes so temptingly arranged at my right hand. This was but the begining of a day of fast for Mrs. Doyle, and the proprietress of the house made at

9

least seven hundred per cent. on the seventy-five cents charged for
that meal. I can safely say no such profit was ever made on viands
placed at my disposal.

Some of the members of our society have had occasion to com-
pete with Mrs. Doyle for the honors of pedestrianism, and I need
only say that she was *then* as ever the winner in the race to the
wharf. Twelve minutes to catch our breath and we were ushered
on board the "Armenia," and soon the clanking of chains and
creaking of machinery inaugurated our trip up the Hudson. Our
attention was first attracted by a colored individual who seemed
to have great concern lest there was some "Irish gentleman aboard
that had been left behind," and by the ringing of what reminded
me of a great dinner-bell wanted us to particularly understand that
this boat tarried not at Tarrytown.

The stewardess, a genuine African, whose hair rivaled her complexion in whiteness, and frizzled most naturally without the appli-
cation of hot irons, perambulated the cabin with smiles on her
Ethiopian visage, and kindness in her heart.

While I shall not enter into any extended guide-book description of the loveliness of the Hudson river scenery, yet I am justly
indebted to its pages for many of my illustrations. If in 1609
Henry Hudson had not made this wonderful discovery for us, the
glory might have been left for some successful female navigator. If
in imagination we wander back to those primitive times, how shall
we compare the perfection of the wildness of the seventeenth century with the perfectness of cultivation of the nineteenth?

How futile must be even my *best* efforts at a description of the
grandeur of this Eden of America upon the one hand, while upon
the other, peak upon peak of cragged rocks rise to such a height
that we may fancy the angels perching upon them as they take
their flight between the two worlds. This river whose beauty and
utility are acknowledged by the whole world, is an offspring of the
Adirondack mountains and bears the likeness of its parents along
its banks for the three hundred miles of its course to the ocean. All
the poetized beauties of the Rhine are monotonous compared to the
ever varying landscape along the Hudson. Not being a German,
we eschew the beer gardens of Hoboken, and the array of breweries
that line the banks and sail soberly on our way. What a shame
that the beauties of nature must, even on historic ground. be marred
by distilleries, propagators of intemperance. At the base of the

Weehawken hills, in 1804, occurred the duel between Alexander Hamilton and Aaron Burr, which resulted in the death of the states-man Hamilton. At Fort Lee begin the palisades, a term applied to a wall of rocks, over twenty miles, along the western bank of the river. They are narrow, being in some places not more than three-quarters of a mile wide. The situation for summer uses is admira-ble, salubrious air and unbounded prospect. While the western shore is one of barren rock, the eastern, in striking contrast, blos-soms out with greenest verdure, fairest flowers, most beautiful villas, an aristocratic display unmarred by a single common feature. Two miles below the town of Yonkers are Mount St. Vincent, and the castle-like residence, now a part of St. Vincent, but formerly the residence of the tragedian, Edwin Forrest. It is a Roman catholic convent school for girls, and while famous for its educa-tional advantages, I trust our western daughters may be free from the pernicious instructions its name suggests. We are told the building is of red brick, certainly not charming to the eye, but as "distance lends enchantment to the view," I found the sight par-ticularly pleasing and the old castle inspired me with feelings of awe. I shall not attempt a description of the various towns we reached, as the appearance of all river towns at the water's edge is unprepossessing, and the visuals orbs are greeted with the backs of tumble-down looking buildings, coal elevators and debris that everywhere line the wharves.

It cannot be expected that a minute description be given of what I have not seen, therefore of Sunnyside, the home of Wash-ington Irving, I remain silent, but on the opposite shore I remem-ber Nyack, and the glimpses of its loveliness, I took in during the brief time allotted me. Tarrytown, twenty-nine miles from New York, Washington Irving tells us was so named by the housewives of the neighboring country, in consequence of the inveterate pro-pensity of their husbands to linger about the village taverns. The name might not be inappropriately applied to some western towns we might mention. The Dutch called it Wheat Town, because of the abundance of that cereal on the hills and valleys around. It seems as if nature had outdone herself at this point, and indeed nothing but elegance greets the eye for miles as we glide along the smooth waters and marvel at the harmonious combination of the works of God and man. With a description of the craft of the Hudson I feel myself totally unable to cope, my knowledge of navigation being limited, and but for the horses I can barely distinguish between a brig and a canal boat. The historic account of Tarrytown is associated with the story of Arnold and Andre. The latter tarried too long on his visit to Arnold, and was arrested on a spot now within the precincts of the town. Washington Irving attended Divine service at this town, Sunnyside being only three miles distant. He lies buried near the old Dutch church at Sleepy Hollow. I would fain claim relationship with this illustrious personage. His mother's name was Sarah.

When we are sweltering under the heat of the sultry days of the summer of 1877, it will be comforting to think that the previous year we passed so near the famous Rockland lake embosomed in the hills near Nyack, from which comes the greater portion of ice used in New York, and probably the largest ice market in the world. One thousand men are employed in cutting and storing ice, some two hundred thousand tons being the annual supply.

Thirty-three miles from New York, Sing Sing with its horrible suggestions looms before our view. Its appellation is derived from the Indian name Ossiving, meaning "stone upon stone." The prison was founded in 1826. The building has been erected by the convicts, of stone quarried on the spot. What may have been the incentive to labor actuating those prisoners while rearing this secure home for themselves, those of us who have never been deprived of our freedom may never know. It has an iron foundry, and manufactories of shoes, whips, saddles and furniture. Thus the covering for our feet may have been made by hands in bondage— the elasticity of the whips their fingers have woven, may have been tried over their own backs, because of their disobedience to prison laws. While their deft hands made firm the leathern saddle-girdle their eyes may have gazed in vain at the hills over which they may never ride, mounted on steeds fleet in their freedom. Even in those prison walls is shown the supremacy of woman, as *her* prison house stands to the east on higher ground, and she whiles away the tedious hours in making clothing. The building for refractory females is of marble and has one hundred and eight cells, while for men twelve hundred cells are prepared, showing in which sex lies the preponderance of perversity.

About four miles above Sing Sing, Croton river enters the Hudson. Six miles up the river is Croton lake, from which New

York city is supplied with water, conducted by an aqueduct, over forty miles long, by sixteen tunnels and over twenty bridges.

At Kidd's point, now called Caldwells' landing, we enter the Highlands. Fifty-one miles from New York is West Point, rightly named so far as our observation serves us, as from the steepness of the rocks, the denseness of foliage, but a point of the beauties of this place is to be seen from the boat landing. I am told love-making is carried on here in the summer season, regularly and harmlessly. In 1812, an act was passed by congress, authorizing the establishment of the Military Academy, on its present broad foundations and its organizations and appointments have steadily improved. No luxuries are permitted, and the students are trained to endure the rigors of the active military life for which they are preparing. This accounts for the harmlessness of the darts of love which are annually hurled at them by the fairest of Hudson's fair daughters. In choosing a husband, I recommend the West Point Cadets to the young ladies as being better prepared for married life, inasmuch as they have not been allowed waiters, horses or dogs, at this military school, and each student is compelled to make his own bed and clean up his own tobacco (for I do not suppose the managers of the institution are so cruel and unmindful of what is so conducive to the health and happiness of man, as to deprive these sons of war of that fragrant, comforting weed.) Lights are darkened at ten and the embryo soldier is supposed to go to sleep. In choosing, be sure you get one that conforms to the rules, for there are intimations that soldiers, like mice, need the vigilant eye of a staid feline to keep them from mischief. The insubordinate ones are known to indulge in what they call "midnight hash" consisting of various edibles mixed in the wash-basin and cooked over a gas stove produced from the chimney. If the current of these convivial spirits is interrupted, the guests decamp and leave the host to explain the confusion. We read that upon the walls of the chapel are tablets bearing the names in gilt letters of the generals of the revolution. Benedict Arnold's has only the words "Major General, born 1840" with furrows in the stone as if the inscription had been cut out. Would that each traitor to our country during this century could have a like mark of opprobrium set upon his memory. The remains of Gen. Winfield Scott rests in the cemetery at West Point. Near this place are two mountains, Storm King, the highest point of the Highlands, 1,800 feet, and Cro'nest, the latter, the scene upon which was founded the charming poem entitled "The Culprit Fay," by Joseph Rodman Drake. The author was then twenty-one, and upon this poem his fame chiefly rests. Idlewild, the home of N. P. Willis is hidden from our view. As a rebuke to the owners of some of the beautiful grounds on the Hudson, who have denied strangers admission to their homes, N. P. Willis says, "Doors may lock, but *out* doors is a freehold to feet and eyes." In this vicinity, I remember, the Hudson river railroad is constructed over the water, and as we were passing, a long train of cars distanced us showing at what a slow rate we were moving compared to the flying iron horse attached to the rail cars. We were in sight of the railroad track the most of our way, and train after train flew past us, and after our weary eyes could gaze no longer, we half wished we were on board the Express bound for Albany.

We pass Newburg, and that enormous bell again rings out and our ubiquitous darkey in stentorian tones thundered out, "The aft gangway for Poughkeepsie." We belie not the meaning of this word as we land in this "safe and pleasant harbor." Near this place is the celebrated woman's college, founded by Matthew Vassar, at which three hundred and fifty young women are educated. The college contains one thousand doors, and certainly there can be no lack of communion in that place. The student of nature can view her works from seven hundred and fifty windows.

At several points along the river we have glimpses of the Catskill mountains stretching into invisible distance beyond the western bank. They rise abruptly from a plain on their eastern side and are ascended by a winding road at the edge of the deep glen, near the head of which is an amphitheatre, inclosed by lofty heights, where Rip Van Winkle fell into his long sleep of twenty years. I had the pleasure of viewing the representation of these mountains at this point, in McVicker's theater, and the celebrated Joe Jefferson personated, as he alone can do, poor Rip and his oft-repented but uncontrollable habit of intemperance. Among these glorious scenes lived Cole, the artist who painted the "Voyage of Life." Catskill Landing is one hundred and eleven miles from New York, on the western shore. The Catskill enters the river, near by, which is navigable for large vessels a mile from its mouth. Here Henry Hudson anchored "The Half Moon," on the 20th of September, 1609.

We are nearing our place of destination, weary in body and mind, for we have carefully followed the beauteous display of nature the whole of the one hundred and forty-four miles from New York to Albany, with the exception of the time devoted to dinner and the unravelling of that bill of fare, the difficulty of which lay in making the prices and our pocket-books harmonize. The soup would have been admirably adapted to irrigating purposes. The half of a roast chicken being sixty-five cents and sold in no less quantity, and having neither time nor inclination for such herculean task, we did not invest in fowl. Before leaving home I was told that I was going into a land of sweet potatoes. Whoever supplies the Hudson river boats with that palatable article must be a millionaire, as for the half of a small potato ten cents is charged, but the deliciousness of the desert over-balanced the defectiveness of the first portion of the meal, the high tariff notwithstanding.

In the after-part of the day the sky became o'erclouded, and our imagination was called upon to supply the warm tints the obscured sun withheld. As evening drew near, had a vision of paradise burst upon me I could not have been aroused from the apathy this surfeiting of beauty had evidently produced, and had it not been for the name of sleeping during a journey on the Hudson, I think I should have fallen into dreamland without an effort. But my fellow-travelers began to gather up their several satchels and bundles, and sleep was denied me, for I must be on the alert lest *my* precious satchel fall into the hands of thieves. If it be true that "As ye judge, so shall ye be judged," it is not a comforting thought to ruminate upon, that during one's travels they are looked upon with a suspicious eye, and instead of being considered innocent till found guilty, it is quite to the contrary and embezzlement is attributed as your besetting sin.

Albany, the city that is said to have existed one hundred years without a lawyer, is reached at last. The plank is thrown out and we endeavor to alight. The pleasures of the day being over, our trials commence. Having seen our baggage properly checked, satchel in hand, we set out on foot for Stanwix Hall, a short distance from the boat landing. All the imps of darkness, fresh from the regions of the furies, could not have besieged us as did the gamins of Albany, intent on relieving us of our hand baggage. Being two lone females in a strange city, we committed ourselves

to the protecting care of a policeman, and succeeded in reaching
the hotel without loss—save that of temper. Deep darkness set
in and heavily the rain drops fell, and we were glad to enjoy
undisturbed the luxuries our rooms afforded. There were two
suspicious looking doors, without bolt or key, leading from our
bedroom besides the one that connected it with our parlor, and
being ever vigilant as to burglars, we secured them by removing
our bedstead in such a manner as to fasten both. We even tightly
closed the transom, and shut ourselves in with feelings of perfect
security and satisfaction—shut in from the turmoil and bustle of
the moving world; shut in from wind and wave and rolling tide;
shut in with our blissful retrospection of all the delights the day
had given us, the rapturous experience, an influence upon our lives
that even four score years and ten may not dispel. Beautiful
Hudson! Smoothly gliding waters. Bear on thy bosom precious,
human freightage, and if on earth our eyes no more behold thee,
in spirit let us' nestle in thy mimic waves or hover among the
green, mossy dells that line thy banks. When the storm king
reigns 'mid the mountains and the barques toss wildly on the
treacherous waters, may that voice still whisper as of old: "Peace
be still."

CHAPTER XX.

ALBANY, a city of over 80,000 inhabitants, is situated on the West bank of the Hudson, "at the head of sloop navigation and near the head of tide-water." In 1623 Fort Orange was built where the city now stands, and next to Jamestown, in Virginia, was the earliest European settlement in the original thirteen states. It is the port of the great Erie canal from the West, which traverses the state from Albany to Buffalo parallel with the railroad, and Champlain canal from the North. The new Capitol when finished will be the largest and most magnificent structure in America, excepting the Federal Capitol at Washington. The city has fifty-four churches. The elements conspire to make Thursday morning, October fifth, one of gloom, but if ever a place looked cheering and inviting to me, it was the breakfast room of Stanwix Hall on that very morning. The bill of fare embraced everything that was most appetizing, and during my two thousand miles journey, the credit of variety, wholesomeness and abundance, together with alacrity in serving, must rest with this house and combine to make that meal one of the most enjoyable of the many taken in public places during my extended tour. The New York Central railroad depot being near our hotel we walked thither while the rain fell in torrents, and once more were en route for a sight of familiar faces. We pass Schenectady, one of the oldest towns in the State of New York, and the road crosses the Mohawk river and Erie canal on a bridge nearly 1,000 feet long. The scenery consists of wild cascades, rapid rivers, and lovely green hills, under which are nestled homes of comfort and elegance. We reach Utica, ninety-five miles from Albany, about noon and take the cars on the Delaware and Lackawanna road going South. Between Utica and Sherburne, our place of destination, I saw a coveted spot where I could rear a home and be happy. From our elevated position on the railway it

10

seemed to be a basin surrounded by wooded hills, itself not devoid
of cranny nooks, slight elevations and indigenous pines, small lakes
and clear streams, green pastures enclosed by symmetrical stone
walls.   There were sloping knolls where orchard trees bore red and
golden fruit.   No bottomless sloughs to engulf the traveller, but
boggy morasses where grows the spicy wintergreen with ruby berry.
Beechnuts and chestnuts to be had for the gathering, and lovely
ferns with no rattlesnakes entwined about their roots as among the
wild flowers of the prairie.   Though by the roadside the sheep
seek sustenance apparently from the gravel stones that thickly strew
their paths, their bleat is reverberated across the waters from hill to
hill and they are content in their native pastures.   Though the
luscious fruit when shaken from its parent stem, rolls a quarter of a
mile distant, it makes all the more merriment for the eager urchins
that stretch out their hands to stop its progress.   Now I catch the
first glimpse I have had for years, of a hop yard, and I am carried
back to those frosty mornings and sweltering days when I helped to
pick the hops of my neighbors, acquiring such digestion thereby, it
seemed as if I could never get satisfied with those palatable viands
among which were delicious rice puddings, so thickly embellished
with raisins that there was one for each mouthful.   If the fat hop-
worms were the ugliest feature in the business, the hop dances were
not among the least of the pleasures, but the crowning glory of the
season was after our labors were o'er and the fragrant hops were
all stored away in the kilns to dry, we took one farewell dance to
the music of our favorite band, "The Whitmore's," and, at a late
hour in the morning, departed for our several homes, rich in health
and also having added something to our financial resources, the
sum being according to the nimbleness of our fingers, however.
We reach Sherburne at nightfall and after some waiting for the
stage, we embark in the primitive manner of the inhabitants of
this portion of the country, ere the iron horse awoke its echoes.   If
we had feared for our personal safety before, when at the dead hour
of night the cars had rushed through the blackness of deep woods
and rocky caverns, or when on board the steamers, we had shuddered at the thought of a fearful explosion, that if it did not immediately land us in eternity would leave us helpless and drowning
in the cold water—, what were our imaginings now as we jolted
over the stony road with the galloping horses, now on the verge of
a ravine whose depths on this cloudy night seemed interminable;

now toiling up some tedious hill, balanced upon its top for a moment and again dashing down its rough declivity or darting over some rude bridge whose loose boards rose up as if to offer an apology for its dilapidated state; these things we endured with only a whispered "Oh!" now and then by way of relief to our surcharged feelings. Yet I can look back upon that seven miles ride with a degree of pleasure for at its termination I stepped under the roof that sheltered my nativity. 'Twas but a little hamlet where it rested, yet its picturesqueness could not be surpassed. Fortified on all sides by the stronghold of nature—her hills, guarded by files of forest giants—her trees, watered by the continued accumulation of the dew drops of heaven—her brooks and rills, inhabited by a peaceful God-fearing people, could one seek a more desirable spot in which to recuperate their expanded energies and throw off the fatigue consequent on a three weeks tour of the world? As the wheels of our vehicle rattle noisily over the gravelly road-bed they aroused the inmates of the little white cottages and lights appeared at the doors and windows and expectant faces peered out into the darkness, for the good natured driver was always in readiness to perform errands for the more ambitious dwellers in this retired spot, and it was no unusual occurrence for a mysterious looking package bearing the ear marks of a more pretentious railroad town, to be dropped into waiting hands and was sure to awaken the curiosity of the next neighbor. On the arrival of the stage coach, this evening, the bundles took a human shape and evidently were expected for no sooner did the rumble of the wheels cease, till a fair young face stood in the doorway and the most musical of voices gave us greeting—such a greeting as is found outside of all the shams of fashionable life—a heart-greeting that shines from the eyes and such warm clasps of the hands that truthfulness lies in each pressure. A bright, warm fire shed a glow of comfort around the spacious living room, and to our chilled limbs was most acceptable. The very air seemed to be filled with welcome written by the fingers of the firelight. The cheery clock ticked out the hour of nine as we ate our vesper meal in the very room where my infant life first received sustenance from the parent breast. Dear mothers! How much patience and suffering they endure for the sake of their offspring—suffering that is never understood till mature years bring its experience. The weariness attendant on the day's journey forbade much communion at that late hour, and we

were shown to a warm sleeping apartment with a downy bed most
inviting. I could close my weary eyes, but not to sleep. Considering the eventful place, sleep must be courted and a true lover's
wooing I gave it, but the thirty odd years of my life each came in
as a witness for a hearing and my cause was on trial far into the
night. How much of my career fell far short of my approbation,
and how I longed to live over some of my youthful days that I
might profit by the experience of after life; and yet I had no dreadful misgivings of conscience for I felt that my faults lay upon the
surface, while within, I carried a loving heart and a will, though
sometimes obstinate, disposed, in the main to perfect obedience to
the mild dictations of my parents. As my head rested on the soft
pillow I thought of my indulgent father whose years were numbered a few months before I had reached the first decade of my life.
His thin, silvery locks seemed again to curl around my fingers as I
tenderly smoothed them away from his white forehead and lovingly
kissed the dear face that was ever full of affection for his "little
daughter." Sitting in my chamber window I could follow the old,
oft trodden path that led to his place of business where he retailed
the little stock of provisions necessary to supply the humble wants
of each family in and around that isolated hamlet, and measured,
yard by yard, the bright prints and rich silks and bombazins that
were the pride of old and young hearts, following fashion's train.
And the sweet, patient face of my mother came back to me, and I
remembered well her resignation and trust in a Higher Power,
when her earthly stay and support was taken from her. When in
the prime of life, her ever busy hands had made tidy this little
home and adorned it with all the skill of which she was capable.
The attractions of her kitchen were its neatness and appetizing
delicacies; those of her parlor, its beauty and absence of all gaudi-
ness. With a serenity of mind to be envied, she reigned queen
over her household gods, beloved at home; respected abroad and no
beggar departed from her door empty handed, and as I now kept
nocturnal vigilance under the roof where she had cared for my
many infantile wants, I thought it not improbable that the same
spirit of wakefulness might be hovering over her couch miles and
miles away in one of Wisconsin's shady glens and thoughts of her
youngest born, wandering o'er the old familiar places, were not
absent from her vigils. The little town slumbered on so peacefully. Most of its inhabitants were aged and with whitened locks,

but steady step awaited calmly the summons that should take them hence to another haven of perfected rest. Though this quiet burgh was not noted for being erected on the spot where were fought the battles of our forefathers, yet in former times, when these aged people were full of youth and before so many of their companions lay down to their long sleep, it was periodically agitated by political strife and natural gossip, born of its inland position and for which there was no outlet. But were this a polar nigh*, the three hundred and fifty-four and one-third hours of its length would be none too long in which to recapitulate the joys and sorrows of the past, and nature's restorer came at last and with it oblivion to earthly ruminations.

CHAPTER XXI.

FRIDAY morning was still dark with clouds and rain and we busied ourselves in re-arranging the much abused garments in our ⟨ranks⟩, giving some of them a much needed bath to remove if possible some of the clayey soil of the Keystone state that adhered with such tenaciousness. Voluble tongues kept pace the while with industrious hands as we converted ourselves into merry washerwomen. There was a fascination in the warm, saponaceous suds and after three weeks of indolence, such vigorous exercise would promote digestion. Our appetites needed no awakening save that produced by those large, mealy potatoes so generously provided, and which we well appreciated after being treated to that soggy under-done vegetable we everywhere found at hotels. A potato to be eatable must have been made subject to sufficient heat to cook it through, which process invariably produces mealiness. Since seeing the bright array of patent cook stoves and ranges at the Centennial, I have hopes that hereafter the traveling public will not be feasted(?) on raw potatoes, but whether baked or boiled in their jackets, they will come to the table bearing some resemblance to the palatable potato served at private dwellings.

Columbus Center, my birthplace, is akin to the great metropolis of New York in as much as it has its "little church around the corner." Its members are Universalists and on the Sabbath, flock thither from over the hills and from out the dells for miles around. This edifice stands just across the street from my early home, and thus was I born under the shadow of the house of prayer, and nourished under the droppings of the sanctuary. Once more I trod its broad aisles and sat in my father's pew cushioned by the hands of my mother. The mattress, with its old-fashioned covering was still in its place, kept as a sacred relic of those who were gone. Again I took my accustomed place in the gallery where the choir was wont to raise one harmonious voice in anthems of praise or chant a solemn requiem over some one more fortunate than the others in having o'erstepped the boundary between the two worlds ere life became a burden or sorrow clouded all joy. Where were my companions? Where the grey heads of the grandsires—where the toddling infants—where the middle-aged— where the pastors? Those still on earth, scattered like autumn leaves; the others garnered in heaven. My voice no longer dared to awaken the echoes of that holy place, but my heart thrilled with thoughts of the past and not one precious face was forgotten. To me their images still occupied the same seats; the eloquent words of the inspired divine that offered such consolation over my father's coffin, still lingered in my ears and the music of the choir still filled the air as the united worship of heart and song went on. I seemed to hear anew the good old hymns of "Orion" and "Balerma" and infused with the inspiration of our beloved pastor I joined in his query:

"While circling worlds shall onward move
    And truths eternal shine.
Shall I through heaven's bright cycle speed
    A human form, divine?"

Softly close the door and shut in the echoes of that sanctuary I may never more awaken. Tread lightly adown those steps

where twenty years before gathered young men and maidens—
my childhood companions whose youth, like mine, may come not
again.

CHAPTER XXII.

ON the corner within range of the church-spire, dwelt our
family physician whose years numbered nearly three-fourths
of a century, and whose experience with the sick and suffering
embraced a period, to my certain knowledge, of over thirty years.
My earliest remembered play-mate was his lovely daughter of the
age of myself. When but scarcely entering the path of maiden-
hood, the angels saw fit to make of her a companion, and father
and mother were bereft of their daughter. The mother never
fully recovered from the blow, and as I looked once more upon
her sad face I saw that her "Mary" was not yet forgotten. The
dear old doctor had lost none of the buoyancy, that was said to be
the secret of his success in his practice, and entertained us with a
mixture of mirth and logic peculiar with him. Across the street
from his home lived a beloved friend of my mother's and as she
opened the door to the daughter of her cherished friend, she took
me to her heart and gave me motherly kisses such as she had
imprinted on my round face in the days of my babyhood. Her
abundant white hair lay in waves and threatened to break out
from the confines of her comb, into the charming ringlets of her
early days. The black eyes had all the brilliancy of youth and
her smile bore the sweetness of sorrow and resignation. Dear
Aunt Sally! even unto old age are you handsome and "unspotted
from the world." My life indeed would be enriched could I live
within reach of your counsel and receive the light of your smile
and profit by your example. May your life, whose purity is as the

crystal waters of the singing brooklet at your door, flow peacefully
on for years yet to come, and may the brightness of your example
remain undimmed long after your ears shall have become deaf to
the music of the little stream as it dashes along its narrow bed.
Another Friday is with the past and at eventide I sit in the parlor
of our hostess, and, accompanied by the piano, sing a dirge over
the death of my childhood, my father and my youth's companions.

CHAPTER XXIII.

SATURDAY, October seventh, was a dismal morning with
its chilly wind and driving rain, but our projected tours
could not be postponed, and after we have a warm combat with
the smoothing iron for an hour or so, the faithful family horse is
brought to the door, and undismayed by the unpropitious elements
we drive over the hills for a day's visit with old friends. Such a
warm welcome as we received everywhere is indescribable, and
quite enough to keep our spirits up and hearts aglow despite the
drenching storm that might well intimidate a more intrepid trio.
Elderly gentlemen and their honest wives embrace us cordially
while the young lambs of the flock are all innocence and sprightli-
ness. There seemed to be a dirth of young men, and I do not
remember to have seen but one young, unmarried man during my
four day's stay in Columbus. This Saturday's dinner table fairly
groaned under its abundance of food and there was nothing to
disturb our happiness but the thought of the impending parting.
After music and song the good bye's were spoken and we departed
feeling that we had left unsaid much that we intended to speak,
but gratified with the sense of having been remembered even unto
the years of womanhood. Sunday morn, October 8th, there was a
fall of snowflakes, prognosticators of the drifts of winter that were

to fill every hollow till earth is one vast sheet of snow and the
level roads have no boundaries for the fence-posts are encased
in white mantles and their heads are no where to be seen.
The faithful horse is again at the door, and, protected by water-
proof, blankets and umbrella we bid defiance to wind and
weather and journey southward. A half mile's travel brings us
to the grave of my father. Everything about the burial-place
bespoke neglect and decay, but the words inscribed on his tomb-
stone "He lives in memory," are still true, for, as green as the
myrtle I plucked from his grave, is the remembrance of our
paternal ancestor in the hearts of his children. We continue our
journey for a distance of five miles when we reach the lovely
village of New Berlin, with its wide streets and rows of shade
trees and homelike dwellings, many of which combine elegance
with simplicity. The joy of again meeting the dear aged face I
sought, must be left for the next world, and disappointed we shape
our course north-ward through the valley of the winding Unadilla, each curve of the road displaying much sequestered loveliness, undisturbed by noise of steam or din of cities. After three
miles more of travel we reach the spot above all others I longed
most to see, not for its splendor, but "Fondest affection that binds
me to thee, my old home, my dear happy home." When I was but
five years of age my father retired from mercantile life and
invested his means in land. I thus became the daughter of a
granger, though no such charming, fanciful appellation concealed
the honorable avocation of farming in those good old days. And
now with the first familiar sight of this dear "Happy Valley,"
my childhood came back to me and I was again a merry, romping
child. Bred to country life, I became one of nature's daughters,
choosing my mates from among her true children; her leafy forest
trees, her butter-cups and daisies, and golden dandelions, her
clover blossoms, her limpid streams; all these in summer. In
winter I reveled in ice and snow and her barren trees were gaunt
specters for the play of my imagination. Twenty years since I
had bidden a tearful adieu to the old homestead. Did I find it
much changed? Yes, there was a change. The *body* was there—
the spirit had flown. Though this cot in the valley I loved, still
nestled under the hillside, and the little stream went murmuring
onward to the river and thence to the sea; though cattle lowed
upon the hilltops and the strong work horses renewed their vitality

11

from the freshly mown meadow lands, they were not the same
that years ago answered to my calls with looks of affection in their
mild eyes and that ate from the store I so willingly set for them.
Parents, brother, sisters, friends—all gone, and I gazed as doth a
mourner o'er the dead, upon what once I fancied would be mine
to enjoy perpetually. Alas! the precious soil was cultivated by
strange hands. The old rooms that once echoed our laughter and
songs, were now occupied and cared for by those to me unknown,
and as I peered into each familiar corner there appeared to me
ghosts of earlier years which my imagination clothed with garments ancient and unique, a supply of which was ever kept in
that glorious old place for solitude and rubbish, the garret. With
that word comes retrospection. With the bright sunshine of each
May, came the yearly renovation of this dusty place, whose ceiling
was festooned with many a cobweb; whose slanting walls were
adorned with various weapons of domestic warfare; whose floor
was covered with huge chests filled with warm, winter blankets.
In one corner was a set of pewter dishes which with unuse were
given to rust that doth corrupt. There was a heavy iron tea-kettle
which my imagination always placed over a roaring fire in my
grand-mother's kitchen before the days of modern cook stoves
and the perplexities of choosing base-burners. How I used to
sing as I brushed the dust from these relics of my predecessors,
and the sound of my voice reverberated among the rafters and
frightened the very rats from their dens and they went scampering
and squealing to more remote corners while I went on with the
rejuvenating of their winter quarters. I was always full of the
cares of a mimic household, the concreteness of its members being
made up of round pumpkins and crooked-necked squashes in
summer, and rags and bran the year through. But one china doll
ever came in my possession, and her smoothe, handsome physiognomy was far too nice for every day wear consequently I clung
tenaciously to a huge rag-baby weighing some eight pounds,
which was never griped with colic, for her digestive apparatus was
of bran. Her cuticle, formed of the strongest muslin, never
underwent that seven year's ordeal peculiar to childhood, that
brings with it the sublime happiness of scratching, the sole cure
for which is fire and brimstone. Her diet was of sufficient abstem-
iousness to suit the most persistent Grahamite. Her hair never
grew much and as such a thing as jute was unheard of in those

early days, and false locks only worn by very aged people, I had
to conceal her hereditary baldness with white lace caps which
added to the attractiveness of her *inky* black eyes and cheeks rosy
as the juice of juniper berries. Such fancy toilets as were designed
especially for her use would drive Worth distracted with envy.
Size indicated nothing relative to the ages of my family. Curious
people seldom had their inquisitiveness gratified when they sought
to pry into my domestic arrangements. It was a model family,
fluctuating numerically between six and a dozen, of all shapes and
sizes, over which I was supreme head and ruler, and none dared
question my management and the perfect control under which I
held my willing subjects. Happy childhood, each child monarch
of a realm over which he reigns with all the tyranny of a fabled
giant, the story-book makes them acquainted with. That fell
destroyer of domestic fowls, the peeps, made such havoc among
my pet turkeys and chickens, and all superfluous kittens met with
such untimely deaths by strangulation in the wash-tub, that it
necessitated my choosing a burial place all silent and beautiful,
befitting a necropolis. I selected a site in one corner of the
orchard on ground gently sloping, near a rickety corn-crib—an
emblem of decay—and noted more for remoteness than artistic
beauty. A pearly brook chanted a requiem in the fence corners
of my grave-yard and the old apple trees dropped their leaves in
autumn as a winding sheet for the dead, while the ripe fruit rolled
to the bottom of the hill, pausing not till it reached the stone wall,
a solid barrier, preventing them from crossing the road and con-
tinuing their course to the river. But I must bid memory depart
and recall the scenes of my journey as they occurred. I followed
the well remembered path up the hillside and climbed the old
familiar rock, upon whose summit I was wont to perch myself at
the close of the summer days when I went in quest of the dear old
cows. There was no boundary to my vision till it encompassed
many miles to the north and south. Its eastern and western
boundary was abruptly terminated by hills one-half mile apart.

This Sabbath day the clouds met with a momentary disperse-
ment and the sun bathed Shacktown pond in a flood of amber
light, and revealed the forests clothed with all the variegated
hues of Autumn. Shacktown, though unromantic in name, was
famous for luscious blackberries that grew there in great abundance, but after their gathering, so dense were the briars that

one's garments were apt to be tattered and torn like a veritable
"shack," as tramps were then denominated. I watched the deep
river winding like the letter "S" in its boundary of our meadow
and I said to myself, here I have raked the fragrant hay—there
dropped the yellow kernels of corn—here gathered the sweet, red
apples; there the bountifully yielding potatoes. Some spots were
reminders of childhood's griefs; others of extremest joy. I
seemed to have lived years in the two hours spent in roaming over
this, to me, hallowed ground. But when I was seated at the
dinner table standing as it did in the same old spot, seated in my
father's accustomed place, a great longing came over me to be
re-united to my kindred, united just as we used to be, and it was
with the utmost effort that I suppressed the sacred tears I cared
not to shed before the eyes of strangers. Farewell, my little valley
home! Childhood was the charm that bound me to thee and that
charm is broken. I have never fancied a home upon the hilltops.
I want to dwell at their base and receive shelter and protection
from wind and storm; but I may nevermore hope for a fruition of
my longings. Though the light of the Orient crowned my infancy,
the spirit of progress is within me and the far outstretching plains
lure me on. Already they have ushered in, and thus far protected
my womanhood and the remainder of my life, like the setting
sun, must declare westward. And now before I close my eyes,
perhaps forever, upon the sweet content and unsurpassed loveliness
resting in this secluded vale, I will make an everlasting sepulcher
fo the early griefs and joys, struggles and achievements of my
youth. Some I will cast into the deep, deep waters of the
Unadilla; for some I will dig a grave at the roots of the sacharine
maple that used to pour forth its sweetest sap to moisten my young
lips; some shall rest on the hilltop; some in the valley; some at
the brooklet's side; but for every wayward deed, duties omitted
and sins committed, let me dig a grave wide and deep under my
mothers bedroom window where I have so often rocked my inanimate progeny, and there in deep penitence make a sacred interment, that when future trials and temptations beset me, I may
think on this little mound covering my misdeeds and childish de-
partures from rectitude, and profiting by dearly bought experience,
avoid the necessity of a future erection of a mausoleum over hopes
blasted and opportunities wantonly neglected. But Oh! the holiest
remembrances of my youth, those early lessons of piety and mo-

rality made efficacious by the exemplary conduct of my parents, let me carry *them* ever with me, and when the sun of my life shall set, to rise no more, may the effect of abiding by such precepts and example, surround my bier with a halo of sweet and tender recollections. Farewell! farewell!

CHAPTER XXIV.

THE county of my birth, Chenango, is separated from Otsego county on the East by the Unadilla river. Its rocks and hills and fertile valleys make a diversity of scenery more pleasant to look upon with an artistic eye, than with agricultural intentions. What is once produced from the stony soil, is preserved with great pains and the least of its products is not allowed to go to waste. Every stalk of corn is carefully cut and shocked and after being husked, the golden ears are stowed away with scarcely the loss of a single kernel, and the stalks are properly stacked for winter fodder for the cattle. The provident farmer always has shelter for his animals during the cold season, and no shivering, half-starved brutes are seen leaning against an apology for a barn, constructed of four perpendicular posts and four horizontal beams on which are laid loose boards covered with wild prairie grass—the model stable of the West. Such catastrophe's are not infrequent as the overturning of a loaded wagon on one of the steep hillsides under cultivation, but though the result may be a complete demolition of vehicle and grain and an extinguishment of the life of the horses, such land disasters are counterbalanced by the natural longevity of the inhabitants of a climate abounding in a salubrious, invigorating atmosphere. The little village of South Edmeston, Otsego county, New York, consists of a few pretentious dwellings, a hotel, a store or two, a small school house which answers the place of seminary, church, lecture room or opera; a romantic old mill and an inevitable blacksmith's shop. This was our nearest town and trading point and is situated "over the river" as we were wont to locate it, and was a mile and a half from our farm. Crossing the beatiful Unadilla from the West, we come upon this lovely nook, fit resort for Summer's fairies and Winter's frost kings. The Eastern hills, covered with beech, pine and chestnut, tower as on impregnable fortress over this little village as if to protect it from Turkish invasion. During the period of years from 1850 to 1856 I remember it as a place of merriment and also many an intellectual feast. The weather-beaten school house, (which was out of our district and therefore only frequented by me as a visitor) often rung with the well-merited applause given the miniature actors as they in turn represented a Cæsar, a William Tell, a Deacon Homespun. Here were held debates participated in by our local intellectual lights which were of no inferior order. The eloquence of T. J. Smith entranced his hearers during a course of lectures given under this lowly roof. Though his voice to earth is silent, I feel that he still moves on in that bright Beyond, his teachings did more to unfold to me, than those of any other minister of the gospel I have since listened to. I remember his promises to watch over the weary ones of earth. Have our giant doubts deterred him from a fulfillment of those vows, or is he silently keeping vigil over our lives and waiting to receive us in that better land whose glories he so well knew how to protray. After the dream of life is ended shall we sit at his feet and learn the wisdom all the intervening years of heavenly companionship have taught him? I tarry over such congenial memories. I must hasten from this rural village in whose infancy some hypochondriac christened "Snailtown," and recrossing the river ascend the Morgan hill nearly a half a mile in length. At its summit we pause and give our steed an opportunity to regain his breath, while we take a bird's-eye view of the glorious landscape below. After our exclamations of delight are exhausted, there is a moment of silent leavetaking of all this beauty so familiar to my youth. The picture will be forever retained, vividly enstamped on my mind as it is, and tenderly, tearfully will I hang it away in the gallery of memory where frequent reflection is a bar to moth and dust that efface with their touch. A last, a fond goodbye! We gently urge our steed a few rods further over the now level road, and the dear, old, red school house is before us, faded with age but having carefully preserved the marks made by the idle hands of refractory juveniles, my companions in the race for erudition. Here in days past my bare feet made their impress in the dust lying at the side of the broad step. The beechnut grove just across the road made deepest shade all the day through for my play house, strong with an unbroken wall of stone, save where we effected an entrance. The doors were small sticks laid from stone to stone and must be lifted when ingress or egress was wanted, and in no wise permitted we a visitor or intruder to step over the barrier of twigs—emblem of the portals to our domiciles. Broken earthenware was patiently carried from home, that our cupboards might not be wanting in a display of costly china. Deep holes were dug in the ground for cellars and luscious mandrakes stored therein in lieu of potatoes. The mandrake leaf served as umbrellas and beechnuts and crinkle-root were choice edibles purchased at the nearest grocery, which was kept in the trunk of a huge tree that had been torn up by its roots leaving a deep hollow for the young merchants to stand in and deliver us the articles necessary for such mimic housekeeping. That umbrageous wood has been devasted by the hand of man, and only black stumps stand as tombstones to mark the place of our play ground. Do not think that play was the acme of our endeavors. Ah! no. There were teachers fierce and masters kind that guarded our educational interests and if there was no perfection in studies, there was no recreative indulgence. As I stood on tiptoe and gazed through the windows at the familiar desks and closets, I almost fancied I saw again the rosy faces of my mates in their old places, and that my own little red hood and warm shawl and loaded dinner basket were lying on the shelves as of old. I regretted that the door was fastened for I longed once more to step under the roof of this Alma Mater. We are prone to think *our* past held all the happiness possible to youth; but perchance the urchins of to-day whose minds are undergoing the formative process that one day shall lead to great knowledge, enjoy as keenly the green, grassy knolls, those famous places for sports and games once our own, and are as proud over their hard earned laurels as they stand at the head of their class, as were we in the halcyon days when to be a man or woman seemed a far off crowning glory of life. Let us leave children to the blissful hallucination that the power and strength of manhood are sufficient to overcome all obstacles and that for full-grown hands there are no hard tasks to perform; for the feet no pitfalls; for the body no weariness; for the brain no doubts and denials; for the conscience no torturings.

CHAPTER XXV.

MONDAY, October ninth, the weather was still dismal, but the rain had ceased. In the afternoon we visit a dear schoolmate of mine, who gave me a cordial greeting, and presided over her cosy home in the country with the ease and quietness of her mother, who used to provide so bountifully and willingly for our childish wants at those happy times in the long ago when I went from school to pass the night with her two black-eyed daughters. Early Tuesday morning our trunks were repacked, strapped and ready for their final destination—home. The stage is bidden to halt and after many *last* good-bye's we retrace our way to Sherburne. The air being very chilly we were glad when at last we were seated in the warm cars speeding our way back to Utica which we reach a little after midday. After a short walk in that neat, quiet city, we reach Steuben Park, and ringing the door-bell at No. 12, we are ushered into the office of a portly doctor who but for his smile of welcome and recognition. I could scarce believe was once the slim, handsome young schoolmaster in our district, who, while reigning monarch at the red school house, turned the heads of the older girls with his sparkling black eyes, and initiated the younger ones, myself among the number, into the mysteries of physiological lore, the basis of the profession he afterward chose. His trials, as a neophyte in his professional career, are over. Success has crowned his efforts and now with a firm belief in the efficacy of the homeopathic treatment, he goes about restoring the sick to health by means of his mild panacea's. His wife was the favored student at the old, red school-house, while he was on duty there. Her womanhood has fulfilled the promise of girlhood. I think I never saw a more beautiful maiden. Such brown eyes under a low, broad forehead, curling auburn hair, rosy cheeks, a mouth that could smile sweetly with approbation or curl its red lips with scorn at those going contrary to her principles of right. But the charm was not wholly in this physical loveliness. There was an intellectual beauty enstamped on every feature, that spoke of a mind stored with imperishable wealth. She gave us greeting to her stately home with mingled pleasure and dignity in her manner. We were shown to our room and after exchanging our travelling garments for less dusty clothing, we descended to the dining-room where a palatable dinner was served. Two lovely children enlivened the board with their presence. The repast ended, we were conducted to the parlors above, where fluent conversation was the order of the evening. Wednesday our host procured a carriage and took us around the city of Utica, which is situated on the South bank of the Mohawk river and is noted for its extensive manufactures and for being the location of the State Lunatic Asylum, the lovely grounds of which we drove over. Though the day was dark and chilly the ride was an enjoyable one and will long be remembered. The dwelling of this worthy physician is a model one in every particular, and it was with deep regret that we left its hospitable roof, and, satchels in hand, accompanied by our hostess, wended our way to the New York Central depot to take the train due at ten o'clock P. M. The last adieu spoken, Mrs. D——, and myself seated ourselves in the depot, endowed, as we supposed ourselves to be, with all the patience of that afflicted, biblical individual of boil notoriety. Alas! our stock of that Christian virtue ran low ere we heard the whistle of the engine at three o'clock in the morning. After five hours of weary waiting, the train of twenty cars rolled slowly into the station and the light of Thursday morning, Oct. 12th, was dawning yet but dimly. The cars were heavily laden and most of them being without stoves we experienced all the frozen horrors of the glacial period occurring long ages ago, when this earth was under the hands of the Infinite, being molded preparatory to becoming a fit habitation for man. A lady, travelling with a bird, was obliged to throw a shawl over its cage to protect it from frost. The breath of the passengers congealed on the window panes forming a cryptography known only to Jack Frost.

12

One daring gentleman circulated a petition which we all signed (save those perhaps whose fingers were too much stiffened with cold, to hold a pencil). The article was designed to be presented for publication and set forth the neglect of the railroad officials to provide for our comfort. I am in doubt about its having achieved the purpose for which it was drafted. As soon as the sun shone out with sufficient warmth, I thawed out a little and was enabled to partake of the lunch with which we had provided ourselves. On this route we passed through Syracuse, one of the largest cities in the state of New York, having a population of 55,000. It contains the most extensive salt manufactories in the United States, and we read that it is famous as the meeting-place of political and other conventions. Batavia, 261 miles from Albany, is the site of the State Institution for the Blind. Rochester is situated on both sides of the Genessee river, seven miles from its mouth in Lake Ontario. It is said to be a lovely city. We reach East Buffalo about noon, and after an hour's waiting take the Erie railroad for Niagara Falls, distant twenty-three miles. The cars stop on the American side, and stepping out on the platform I beheld a tall individual with a most melancholy, disappointed look that at once aroused my sympathies, and rushing up to him, I began to offer words of consolation. He embraced me warmly, all travel-stained as I was, and began to utter something about my being his Ruth, and I hastened to inform him after the Bible plan, " Whither thou goest, I will go." I beckoned to Mrs. D——, and gathering up our luggage we three took an omnibus and crossing Niagara river on the suspension bridge we soon arrived at the Prospect House on the Canada side. But pardon me. I have neglected to introduce you to our escort, now smiling and happy and—my husband. We soon satisfied our gastronomical wants at the rate of a dollar per head. There was nothing palatable about that dinner but the cakes and confectionery. When it was ended we sought the Falls and realized all that had been said and written in praise of this wonderful cataract. We lean over the cliffs as far as our courage will allow, and wonder what fascination there is in the mighty rush and roar that lures people to leap into its foaming depths. Is not the love of life paramount to overcome the temptation of self-destruction? Is there no power in the sublimity of such a scene to counteract the delusion that there is rest beyond an act so sinful? As I listen to the awful roar and gaze upon the torrent of rushing waters like a mass of green, molten glass, where it is deepest, I am charmed and awed and lost to all else about me till I feel the grasp of the strong hand of my newly found partner who leads me up the hillside that we may take a survey of all this grandeur from a lofty height. At evening we cross the suspension bridge on foot in order to get a more protracted view. At dark we take the cars again for East Buffalo where we wait in a crowded depot till a late hour for the train that is to take us to Detroit, on the Grand Trunk railway.

CHAPTER XXVI.

FRIDAY morning, October 13th, finds us whirling through Canada, apparently a barren region of country with but few habitations, but abounding in tall straight trees, set so thickly, they reminded me of a hop-yard in spring-time after the setting of the poles. At Port Huron we crossed the St. Clair river. The cars are run onto a ferry-boat and while I thought we were making a very tedious stop we were being ferried gently over the river. Sometime during the journey of the night previous, our old friends Mr. & Mrs. B——, re-joined us and we were happy to see their faces again and learn that they had been enjoying themselves among friends residing in the lovely region of Rochester. We get a glimpse of Lake Huron lying calmly in the sunlight. One would never imagine its hidden waves lashed to the fury of destruction. That portion of Michigan through which we passed before reaching Detroit, resembles the country we saw in Canada. We arrive at Detroit about noon and are huddled into a small waiting-room under the depot roof, and a policeman warningly suggests pick-pockets and watching of our baggage. Mrs. D——, my husband and myself take a short stroll along an unprepossessing street near the river, but we are too tired to appreciate anything in nature and joining Mr. & Mrs. B——, at the depot, we concluded to take the afternoon train for Jackson, thereby making a break in the tedious waiting, so that it should not all be endured at one place. That portion of country is not noted for

much beauty till we reach Jackson. There we again part company with Mr. & Mrs. B——., their intention being to visit other
friends in Michigan. We partake of a much relished supper
served in the depot building, and about nine o'clock in the evening
we take the Michigan Central railroad and passing through the
southern part of Michigan, reach Chicago about six o'clock, A. M.,
Saturday morning, after a long night's ride. Occupying the seat
behind us was our acquaintance of the petition notoriety, from
Utica to Buffalo. Once at Chicago, the anxiety attendant on
feeling that we are almost at home takes possession of us and
leaving Mrs. D——, to the hospitalities of her friends we depart
on the Illinois Central railroad, about nine A. M. While the car
wheels whir and rattle, awakening the echoes of the vast prairies,
we will take a review of Chicago, the principal city of Illinois.
"Within forty years it has grown from a small Indian trading
station to the position of the metropolis of the North-west and
the greatest railway centre on the Continent. It is situated on the
west shore of Lake Michigan, at the mouth of Chicago river. The
site of the business portion is fourteen feet above the lake. It
was originally much lower, but has been filled up from three to
nine feet since 1856. The city stands on the dividing ridge
between the basins of the Mississippi and the St. Lawrence, is
surrounded by prairie stretching several hundred miles south,
west and north. Chicago river and its branches afford a water
frontage of thirty-eight miles of which twenty-four are improved,
without including the lake front, on which an outer harbor is now
in process of construction. The city extends north and south
along the lake about eight miles, and west from the lake about
five miles. The river divides the city into three districts known as
the North, South and West Divisions which are connected by
thirty-three bridges and two stone tunnels under the river bed,
costing $400,000 and $549,000. The streets are generally eighty
feet wide and many of them from three to seven miles long. The
first permanent settlement of Chicago was made in 1804, during
which Fort Dearborn was built by the United States government.
It was abandoned in 1812, rebuilt in 1816 and finally demolished in
1856. At the close of 1830 Chicago contained twelve houses and
three "country" residences in Madison Street, with a population
of about one hundred. Local estimates placed the population in
1875 at 400,000." In October, 1871, Chicago was the scene of a

terrible conflagration commencing Sunday evening, October 8th, in a small barn on DeKoven Street, in the south part of the West Division. The rumor ran that Mrs. O'Leary had a cow, and that bovine had a refractory hind foot, which, forming a coalition with a lighted kerosene lamp so puffed up with gas that it was on the verge of bursting of its own volition, setting aside the velocity and friction of the hoof, caused a combustion of animal and mineral matter, whose effect is unparalleled in all past ages. As neither the cow nor the lamp have since been heard from, is it asking too much of human credulity to believe that the two, small satallites of Mars, lately discovered, are other than those two unfortunate earth-objects, now made heavenly bodies, revolving in space; the one a paradise full of the "milk of human kindness;" the other, since the original Hades is lost to the sight of our more progressive divines, developed into a fiery region of ever consuming petroleum, a fit, final repository for the wicked, whose punishment shall be *eternal*, saith the Lord? The "Origin and Destiny of Man," is a theme that agitates the minds of the deepest thinkers. The origin and destiny of two soulless objects that can cause a conflagration of two day's duration, and whose smoke arose over the ruins for months afterward, may well incite us to speculation on the animate and inanimate forces of nature. But to return to first principles. There were over seventeen thousand buildings destroyed in that fire; 98,500 persons made homeless, and about two hundred killed. The total loss was estimated to be $190,000,000 of which over $40,000,000 were recovered in insurance. Many Insurance Companies failed and thus the loss was damaging to city and country alike. Business soon revived and the indefatigable energy of the merchants soon placed them in extemporized buildings where trade went on as before the calamity. The new buildings are far superior to those burned, and the vestiges of the fire have departed. July 14th, 1874, another fiery blast swept over sixty acres of the city, in its very heart and about four million dollars of property were consumed. The commerce of Chicago ranks second to New York. It has the greatest grain and stock market in the world. The hotels are unequaled. The Palmer House is of iron and brick, and fireproof. The Grand Pacific is built of stone and is six stories high. Wabash Avenue contains the finest residences. A new Court House is being erected at an estimated cost of two million dollars.

The Chamber of Commerce is one of the finest buildings of the kind in the world. Here meets the Board of Trade and the wranglings of its members are said to surpass in noise, the gabble of an old-fashioned quilting party. An enchanting place is McVicker's Theatre. There have I witnessed the tragic acting of Booth as Richard III, and Joe Jefferson in Rip VanWinkle. Hooley's is a smaller Theater, but very beautiful, and there I saw the handsome Lawrence Barrett in the Merchant of Venice. We read that there are about one hundred and eighty churches in Chicago. I attended High Church where the service is chanted. The ceremony is wanting in sacredness conducted in that manner and the Episcopal service is really impressive, I think, when it is read. At Dearborn Observatory there is a Clark refractory telescope, one of the largest in the world. There are six medical Colleges in Chicago, the most noted of which is Rush Medical College, founded in 1842. I was charmed with Lincoln Park, with its 250 acres beautifully laid out; its five miles of drives and walks; its quiet after the heat of the city. Union Park contains seventeen acres and the expenditures thereon are said to be $100,000. The Water Works are a sight worth visiting, with the huge engines revolving and shining like silver. When one has climbed the 130 feet necessary to reach the top of the tower, he is naturally too much out of breath to appreciate the fine view of lake and city, till he has shut his eyes for a moment to keep out the vast expanse awaiting inspection. The tunnel was begun in 1864 and completed in 1866, costing over $315,000. There are forty artesian wells in the city. A certain spiritual medium prophesied in 1864 that oil would be found at the intersection of Chicago and Western Avenues, but although being a false prophet, great good was evolved as the prophecy led to the sinking of the first two wells, one 911 the other 694 feet deep. The Union Stock Yards comprise 345 acres, of which one hundred are in pens, and have thirty-one miles of drainage, seven miles of streets and alleys, 2,300 gates, and costs $1,675,000. There are fifteen grain elevators in the city. Pork packing is conducted on scientific plans, and the squeals of a lively pig are lost to earth in the twinkling of an eye. The Tivoli Garden is the place for choice refreshments and an induction into the arts of table coquetry. The Exposition building is of iron and glass, and is situated in Lake Park. It is but one gem in a crown of jewels compared to the spacious structures of the Centennial Exposition.

CHAPTER XXVII.

O N reaching Gilman, distant from Chicago about seventy-five miles, we make a short stop at the Redfield Hotel while we brush the dust from our garments and endeavor to make ourselves something like presentable before reaching home and friends. As we set foot on board the T. P. & W. train once more, we exclaim with thankfulness, "this is our last change of cars." When the conductor asked for my ticket, I made the request that the last fragment—the heading—be left with me as a souvinor of the eventful year 1876. For us there are no more adieux—nothing but greetings await us as the train speeds us swiftly but safely—home. We are reminded of our long absence by being asked if we wish to be shown to a hotel on alighting on the platform at our station. Have we grown a century older? No: the hotel has changed hands in our absence and the porter mistakes us for some distinguished travelers from the Eastern Continent, no doubt being impressed with our foreign air. We inform him that we *own* a hotel in this thriving village and with a puzzled countenance he leaves us to the tender mercies of our own servants, and *they* being none other than our two selves, go as inclination bid, each serving the other with a right good will, dwelling together through the mercy of God and loving kindness. The first arms around my neck were those of my mother, she having departed from Wisconsin a few days previous to our arrival in Illinois. Her blue eyes were full of affection and pride as I gave her a synopsis of my travels and delivered to her the messages of love and remembrance of which her companions in the East had made me the bearer. I told her of the hearts yet true and tender—of the many landmarks still unchanged, of the lonely grave of our father—of how high the hills towered—how green were their pines; of the sheltering rocks, of how the brooks sang; of how her birthplace, just across the Unadilla from our old home, still slept in the shadows of the chestnut tree under whose branches she played when a child. Tears and smiles went alter-

nately as I recounted all these things yet so vivid in her mind.
Dear, precious mother! May your life be long spared to your children to whose homes your presence brings light and cheer! Next
came the embrace of a sister whose kindness is unceasing, and
dear, little, brown-eyed, auburn-haired Lilly, with a sprinkling of
some of the same naughty freckles that mar the features and tran-
quility of the aunt who loves her best. The tall, rosy-cheeked
brother, though less demonstrative by far, and teeming with classic
lore, came in for a greeting whose warmth was only to be indulged
in after long absence. Home! Let the four letters be engraved in
gold—encircled with costly diamonds and enriched by all precious
gems. What word more sweet; what more the embodiment of
rest and peace. Without homes we are miserable wanderers
seeking contentment and finding it not. Let us make our homes
sacred repositories of loving kindness, true affection and implicit
trust, for having these three, a world of happiness is ours to enjoy
here below, and above, a heavenly mansion already prepared for
our acceptance.

> "This earth hath treasures fair and bright,
>   Deep buried in her caves;
> And ocean hideth many a gem
>   Neath its blue and curling waves.
> Yet, not within its bosom dark
>   Or 'neath its dazzling foam,
> Lies there a treasure equaling
>   A world of love at home."
>
> "True sterling happiness and joy
>   Are not with gold alloyed,
> Nor can they give a pleasure like
>   A merry, home fireside.
> I envy not the man who dwells
>   In lordly hall or dome,
> If midst those splendors he hath not
>   A world of love at home."
>
> "The friends whom time hath proved sincere,
>   'Tis they alone can bring
> A sure relief for hearts that droop
>   Neath sorrows heavy wing.
> Though care and sorrow may be mine
>   As down life's path I roam,
> I'll heed it not if still I have
>   A world of love at home."

www.ingramcontent.com/pod-product-compliance
Lightning Source LLC
Chambersburg PA
CBHW031439270326
41930CB00007B/789